Holy Moments

A Study Of
Burning Bush Experiences

William C. Bartlett

CSS Publishing Company, Inc., Lima, Ohio

HOLY MOMENTS

Scripture quotations are from the *New Revised Standard Version of the Bible*, copyright
1989 by the Division of Christian Education of the National Council of the Churches of
Christ in the USA. Used by permission.

For more information about CSS Publishing Company resources, visit our website at
www.csspub.com.

ISBN 0-7880-1803-5   PRINTED IN U.S.A.

Dedicated
to
Cindy, my wife,
and
Kari and Derek,
my children,
with whom I continue to
experience Holy Moments in Christ

Table Of Contents

Holy Moment Menagerie

Noticing Life's Holy Moments

Think back over your life. Have there been events, people, and circumstances which have profoundly affected you? Can you recall a few *burning bush* moments when you felt as though you were standing on holy ground because the Lord was revealing Himself to you in a way that you knew was going to alter the direction of your life? After encountering these events, people, or circumstances, you were a changed person.

Perhaps one such watershed event was a first-grade teacher whom you loved — because she first loved you with the love of Jesus Christ that radiated through her. She not only taught you as a teacher, but as a mentor and hero she influenced you in ways that she never realized — maybe in ways you never realized, until later — perhaps even now — when you see in your life a perspective and quality that is there because of her.

Maybe another life-changing influence was "church." No, not the building, not even the individual people. Rather, maybe it was the collective experience of growing up in the church:

- the Sunday School openings in the social hall,
- the times you sat in church (not knowing or caring what was going on except that you were next to your mom or dad and you knew something "holy" was going on — whatever "holy" was!),
- the confirmation classes,
- the youth activities,
- the Christmas and Easter worship services,
- the visitation of elderly,
- and the prayers (that you knew were good for you even if you didn't pay attention to them all the time).

Maybe this experience of the "church" affected you more deeply than you consciously ever thought possible.

Or, perhaps it was an illness with which you struggled, or a tragedy you experienced, or a breaking up of a family — your family — that wounded you and opened you up to God's grace in

Christ in ways that you might not otherwise have been open to receive. Throughout the ordeal, in the midst of all the changes you encountered, you clung to (or maybe, you were clung to by) a peace and strength that formed an immoveable foundation which still undergirds your life and world view.

Holy Moments are visitation moments — moments when the Lord visits us directly or indirectly, through events, people, or circumstances for the purpose of shaping us, cradling us, and changing us more and more into His desire for us. Holy Moments leave us changed, affected, redirected, sometimes happier, sometimes pondering, but always holier. "I am confident of this, that the one who began a good work among you will bring it to completion" — one Holy Moment at a time — "by the day of Jesus Christ" (Philippians 1:6).

The Bible is full of Holy Moments. Remember when Moses came upon the burning bush on the mountain? He was even told that it was a Holy Moment, "Come no closer! Remove the sandals from your feet, for the place on which you are standing is holy ground" (Exodus 3:5).

Remember the Holy Moment that occurred on the night of the Passover when the angel of death passed over Egypt and the first-born of every non-blood-marked home died. Remember Elijah's pity-party followed by the Holy Moment of the "still quiet voice" of the Lord. Remember Good Friday, Easter morning, Easter evening. Remember the eerie half-hour silence in Heaven spoken about in John's Revelation, chapter 8.

We do not have to just remember Holy Moments in the Bible; Holy Moments still happen when we read the Bible and experience the amazing grace, the lavish mercy, and inimitable peace that greets us as we encounter the holy gospel of Jesus Christ in the written Word of God.

We all have Holy Moments. Our Lord is active in all of our lives. A goal of this book is to make us all more sensitive and alert to Holy Moments when they happen. Whether we recognize them or not, Holy Moments affect and change us all. Recognizing them allows us to celebrate our Lord's activity in our lives and to find peace and salvation in that saving activity.

The two goals of this book are (1) to testify to Holy Moments that have taken place in the Bible and in my life, and (2) to sensitize you, the reader, to Holy Moments that are occurring, by God's grace, in your life so you may know and believe in Jesus Christ as your Lord and Savior.

At the end of this volume, I have shared two "top ten" lists. First, the ten greatest frustrations that I have experienced over my 22 years of parish ministry. Frustrations are not to be equated with "detestable activities." I still love many of the activities and ministries described in the "Ten Greatest Frustrations" list, but I am still, to this day, frustrated by these challenges. My goal is to so offer these frustrations to the Lord that they become joys. The "Ten Greatest Joys in Ministry" is a list of deeply satisfying activities in parish ministry. I remember once hearing that Mother Teresa was once bandaging the wounds of a leper. A western reporter was observing her and interviewing her at the same time. The reporter, being repulsed at the sight and smell of the leprous appendages, commented, "Ma'am, I would not do that for a million dollars." Without missing a winding in the bandage, Mother Teresa said, "Neither would I." These Ten Greatest Joys are what keep me getting back in the pulpit every Sunday, preparing for another confirmation class thinking "Maybe this will be the one!" and thinking that ministry is the greatest privilege in the whole world!

Finally, in the last chapter, I added a list of some of my memory verses. I love memory verses. Memorizing scripture helps me hide God's Word in my heart (Psalm 119:11) for times when I need it most — often when I'm not around church or a Bible! My hobby of memorizing scripture began while on a family vacation a number of years ago. We had finished "car bingo," the food supply was short, and we had miles to go before we were going to stop. So, we began memorizing one verse from each book of the New Testament.

By the end of our vacation that year, I had 66 passages selected — one from each book of the Bible. I didn't pick out just the shortest verse; every passage I selected was selected because it carried special meaning for me. To keep these verses fresh in my mind, I recite these verses once a week during one of my morning jogs. This helps me obey 1 Peter 3:1: "... in your hearts sanctify Christ as Lord. Always be ready to make your defense to anyone who demands from you an accounting for the hope that is in you; yet do this with gentleness and reverence."

This book is written because of Holy Moments and with the prayer that you will experience many Holy Moments as you grow in the grace and knowledge of your God and Father through our Lord Jesus Christ!

Holy Moments In Scripture

Chapter 1
The Burning Bush

*Moses was keeping the flock of his father-in-law
Jethro, the priest of Midian; he led his flock beyond the wilderness, and came to Horeb, the mountain of God. There the angel of the Lord appeared
to him in a flame of fire out of a bush; he looked,
and the bush was blazing, yet it was not consumed.
Then Moses said, "I must turn aside and look at
this great sight, and see why the bush is not burned
up." When the Lord saw that he had turned aside
to see, God called to him out of the bush, "Moses,
Moses!" And he said, "Here I am." Then he said,
"Come no closer! Remove the sandals from your
feet, for the place on which you are standing is
holy ground."*   — Exodus 3:1-5

Moses was content. No more palatial surroundings of Pharaoh's
palace in Egypt, just the pastoral hills of the Midian countryside.
No more regal feasts with the Pharaoh's court, just family gatherings with his father-in-law Jethro and the rest of the in-laws. No
more prestige and power which elevated him over the rest of his
people, just the humble duty of tending sheep. Moses was now in
his eighties and ready for a quieter life. Moses found this quiet life
with his wife named Zipporah and a son named Gershom.

Do you remember the last time you were as content as Moses
finally found himself? Perhaps the final exams finally ended. Or
the wedding plans flowed smoothly and the wedding day came
and went — beautifully. Perhaps you finally received that promo-
tion, moved to a new city, found great schools for your children,
and built the house of your dreams.

Enter burning bush! The Lord told Moses he was on "holy
ground." Moses knew it — for he was experiencing a "Holy Moment." Moses hid his face — both out of reverence for the Lord

and perhaps wishing that this Holy Moment were not occurring. Moses knew that Holy Moments were life-changing moments.

Moses tried to water down the Holy Moment.

"Who am I that I should go to Pharaoh?" (Moses knew who he was — a wanted man back in Egypt!)

"What if the Israelites ask me Your Name?"

"What if they don't believe me or listen to me?"

"Oh, Lord, I have never been eloquent."

"Please send someone else."

A moment is "holy" when the Lord decides it is to be holy, not when we are in the mood for a "Holy Moment." So Moses' quiet and content life as a shepherd and family man in Midian came to an end as he stood before a burning bush on Mount Horeb. You know the rest of the story (if not, read Exodus).

Be on the lookout for burning bushes in your life. They probably won't be actual burning bushes. Instead, in the midst of the ordinary (as ordinary as a common old bush on Mount Horeb), the Lord will come to you. You will know when the holy breaks into the ordinary. If you don't recognize it, the Lord will inform you that you are at that moment standing on holy ground in the holy presence of Almighty God.

Don't try to weasel out of the holy assignment the holy Lord is giving to you during that Holy Moment. Moses tried. He didn't get far. Excuse me; he did go far — but not in the direction Moses had in mind.

In spite of his initial reluctance, Moses recognized a Holy Moment in this burning bush. He obeyed because he loved the Lord. He went back to Egypt — from where he had fled forty years earlier. He went not because he wanted to go, but because the Lord asked him to go.

Questions

1. Can you think of any ordinary circumstance in which the Lord has ever spoken directly to you, asking you to do something very specific?

2. Have you ever made excuses, trying to weasel your way out of being conscripted into the Lord's service?

3. Recall a time the Lord called you out of contentment into discipleship for His Kingdom.

4. Do you feel the heat of a burning bush near you right now?

Prayer

Almighty God, just as the hearts of the disciples burned within them as they unknowingly talked with their Risen Savior on that first Easter afternoon, so we pray that we would recognize burning bushes in our lives that call us out of times of contentment and into opportunities of serving You and offering freedom from bondage to sin. We ask this in the Name of Jesus Christ, the Lamb of God. Amen.

Chapter 2
The Passover

Tell the whole congregation of Israel that on the tenth of this month they are to take a lamb for each family, a lamb for each household ... Your lamb shall be without blemish, a year-old male; you may take it from the sheep or from the goats. You shall keep it until the fourteenth day of this month; then the whole assembled congregation of Israel shall slaughter it at twilight. They shall take some of the blood and put it on the two doorposts and the lintel of the houses in which they eat it ... This is how you shall eat it: your loins girded, your sandals on your feet, and your staff in your hand; and you shall eat it hurriedly. It is the passover of the Lord. For I will pass through the land of Egypt that night, and I will strike down every firstborn in the land of Egypt, both human beings and animals; on all the gods of Egypt I will execute judgments: I am the Lord. The blood shall be a sign for you on the houses where you live: when I see the blood, I will pass over you, and no plague shall destroy you when I strike the land of Egypt.
— Exodus 12:3, 5-7, 11-13

It seems so cruel. A little lamb. Innocent. What had it done? And, not just one lamb, but hundreds, thousands of lambs. Unfair, unjust, repulsive.

Such, perhaps, were the thoughts of God's people 3,400 years ago on that night of the Passover that freed the Hebrew people from slavery and bondage in Egypt. Such, for certain, are our thoughts as we read in God's Word the account of that crucial (isn't that word, "crucial," related to the latin word for "cross"?) event in the Old Testament book of Exodus.

Moses had gone to Pharaoh ten times prior to this event asking for the freedom of his fellow Israelites. Pharaoh wavered between outright denial of the request to at first granting permission, but then later changing his mind. Finally, the Lord decided the time was right. Pharaoh was given the warning; the Israelites were given the directions. The lambs were given as a sacrifice. The Egyptians were given the shock of their lives. At midnight, the firstborn of every family, every flock, and every felon fell dead.

It was a Holy Moment for the Israelites. How could a little blood on their doorposts spare them the horror of death? How could a little blood from an innocent lamb spare them from death, free them from slavery, and fill them with holy joy?

This Holy Moment didn't last long. They fled — still meticulously following the Passover directions, taking with them unleavened bread and heading out of town. Where were they going? They did not know; but they did know that they had better go. God's Word was true.

It still seems so cruel. A little lamb. Innocent. What had it done? And, not just one lamb, but hundreds, thousands of lambs. Unfair, unjust, repulsive. Yet, such a sacrifice, meticulously planned by Almighty God, freed the people from slavery.

The "crux" of the matter was the blood shed. The real "crux" of the Exodus is in Who the lamb foreshadowed — Jesus Christ on the Cross. Fourteen hundred years later, another Lamb was sacrificed to mark a people with the blood and to free them from bondage. That, too, seemed cruel and unfair. Yet, that sacrifice is the one that also frees us from bondage to sin, death, and the power of the devil.

The Holy Moment of Christ's sacrifice occurred just once, but the Holy Moments of our recognizing the Lamb sacrificed, receiving the offered blood, and following the Call of our Lord still happen at Holy Communion week after week for those who believe.

Questions

1. Why do some people think it so cruel that innocent lambs were slain at the Exodus to free an ancient people from slavery and

yet so cavalierly speak about Christ's sacrifice on the Cross to free us from sin?

2. Is the "crux" of your faith and your local church's ministry the one and only Cross of Jesus Christ? How so? If not, what can you do about it?

3. After recognizing the Holy Moment of the Passover at midnight, the Hebrew people were not only ready, they obeyed the Lord and left town! How will you follow the Lord's lead the next time you celebrate the Passover of the Body and Blood of Jesus Christ at Holy Communion?

Prayer

O Christ, Thou Lamb of God, who takes away the sin of the world, have mercy on us! May we never again receive Holy Communion, the Body and Blood of Christ, without recognizing in it the Holy Moment of Christ's payment on the Cross in our place for our forgiveness, life, and salvation. We ask this in the Name of Jesus Christ, the Lamb of God, who was slain and whose blood was shed so that we might be freed. Amen.

Chapter 3
"We Don't Know What To Do"

"O our God, will you not execute judgment upon
them? For we are powerless against this great mul-
titude that is coming against us. We do not know
what to do, but our eyes are on you." Meanwhile
all Judah stood before the Lord, with their little
ones, their wives, and their children. Then the spirit
of the Lord came upon Jahaziel son of Zechariah,
son of Benaiah, son of Jeiel, son of Mattaniah, a
Levite of the sons of Asaph, in the middle of the
assembly. He said, "Listen, all Judah and inhab-
itants of Jerusalem, and King Jehoshaphat: Thus
says the Lord to you: 'Do not fear or be dismayed
at this great multitude; for the battle is not yours
but God's.' "   — 2 Chronicles 20:12-15

When was the last time you felt like Jehoshaphat, King of Judah,
as he was surrounded on all sides by "multitudes" coming against
him? Read again the last half of 2 Chronicles 20:12: "For we are
powerless against this great multitude that is coming against us.
We do not know what to do, but our eyes are on you."

Have you felt like this recently? Powerless against the multitude that is coming against you? For King Jehoshaphat, it was not
just the multitude of one enemy with lots of troops. It was several
multitudes, each with lots of troops. The Moabites, Ammonites,
and Edomites were all attacking at one time — each from a different direction!

How often does it seem that "multitudes" are coming against
us? The demands of our children seem like an attacking army of
Moabites. The persistent pleas for service from church and school
seem like an army of Ammonites desiring to steal our time. Add to
this the relentless pressure from our bosses and jobs. We join

Jehoshaphat in crying out to the Lord, "We are powerless against this great multitude, Lord. O God, we do not know what to do!"

Notice that Jehoshaphat's prayer did not end there. One more line. *Our eyes are on you!* That was enough! That defined the Holy Moment. That's all the Lord wanted to hear.

God Almighty spoke: "Do not fear or be dismayed at this great multitude; for the battle is not yours but God's."

And, indeed, the battle was the Lord's. They survived. They not only survived; they thrived. Why? Their eyes were on the Lord!

Questions
1. Read Hebrews 12:1-2. As we keep our eyes fixed on Christ, what are we to cast aside?

2. When was the last time you were paralyzed into inaction because you were being pressured from so many different directions? Did you keep your eyes on the Lord? Did you recognize that happening as a Holy Moment?

3. How can we give our battles to the Lord rather than try to fight them ourselves?

Prayer
Lord God Almighty, we fear and tremble about so many things in this world. Lord, one thing is needful in the midst of all the pressures that surround and press against us — and that is to keep our eyes on You. For the real battle is not ours to fight. We ask this in the Name of Jesus Christ, Your Son, our Lord. Amen.

Chapter 4
"There are 7,000...."

Elijah answered, "I have been very zealous for the Lord, the God of hosts; for the Israelites have forsaken your covenant, thrown down your altars, and killed your prophets with the sword. I alone am left, and they are seeking my life, to take it away." Then the Lord said to him, "Go, return on your way to the wilderness of Damascus; when you arrive, you shall anoint Hazael as king over Aram. Also you shall anoint Jehu son of Nimshi as king over Israel; and you shall anoint Elisha son of Shaphat of Abel-meholah as prophet in your place. Whoever escapes from the sword of Hazael, Jehu shall kill; and whoever escapes from the sword of Jehu, Elisha shall kill. Yet I will leave seven thousand in Israel, all the knees that have not bowed to Baal, and every mouth that has not kissed him." — 1 Kings 19:14-18

When was the last time the Lord abruptly interrupted your pity-party?

Elijah was a great and mighty prophet. He stood alone with the Lord against 450 prophets of Ba'al on Mount Carmel. In the end, he stood victorious. King Ahab and Queen Jezebel wanted to get rid of this "troubler of Israel." Elijah ran for his life. Leaving his servant behind, Elijah went into solitary depression (a very dangerous thing for anyone to do). Sitting under a broom tree, he lamented to God, "Take my life."

The Lord was compassionate. The Lord fed him, gave him rest, and touched him through an angel. Elijah was strengthened, but still despondent. He mourned: "I have been very zealous for the Lord, the God of hosts; for the Israelites have forsaken your covenant, thrown down your altars, and killed your prophets with

21

the sword. I alone am left, and they are seeking my life, to take it away."

The Lord then spoke to Elijah — not in the wind, earthquake, or fire. But in a *still, small voice*, defining a Holy Moment, the Lord said, "I will leave seven thousand in Israel, all the knees that have not bowed to Ba'al, and every mouth that has not kissed him."

Elijah was not alone! There was an army of at least 7,000 who were yet faithful!

The next time you are in the midst of a pity-party, remember this passage. You are not alone. Not only is the Lord with you (Matthew 28:20), but there are yet 7,000 others also working for the King of kings. And remember the time when Elijah (with the Lord) stood alone against the 450 prophets of Ba'al at Mount Carmel. The battle is the Lord's!

Questions
1. When was the last time you were really depressed?

2. When was the last time you felt that you were utterly alone in some matter?

3. Name at least seven people whom you know who are faithful disciples of Jesus Christ.

Prayer
Almighty God, Gracious Lord, King of kings and Author of all hope, we praise and thank You for Your faithfulness, goodness, and mercy. Please keep coming to us, Lord. Remind us of Your promises and power. Let us never be afraid. Let us never lose hope in the midst of our self-pity. Instead, Lord, keep coming to us. Sustain us. Feed us. Speak to us through Your still, small voice and through scripture, reminding us that, indeed, Your kingdom is coming. Amen. Come, Lord Jesus!

Chapter 5
Early Morning In Bethlehem

Joseph also went from the town of Nazareth in Galilee to Judea, to the city of David called Bethlehem, because he was descended from the house and family of David. He went to be registered with Mary, to whom he was engaged and who was expecting a child. While they were there, the time came for her to deliver her child. And she gave birth to her firstborn son and wrapped him in bands of cloth, and laid him in a manger, because there was no place for them in the inn. In that region there were shepherds living in the fields, keeping watch over their flock by night. Then an angel of the Lord stood before them, and the glory of the Lord shone around them, and they were terrified. But the angel said to them, "Do not be afraid; for see — I am bringing you good news of great joy for all the people: to you is born this day in the city of David a Savior, who is the Messiah, the Lord. This will be a sign for you: you will find a child wrapped in bands of cloth and lying in a manger." And suddenly there was with the angel a multitude of the heavenly host, praising God and saying, "Glory to God in the highest heaven, and on earth peace among those whom he favors!" When the angels had left them and gone into heaven, the shepherds said to one another, "Let us go now to Bethlehem and see this thing that has taken place, which the Lord has made known to us." So they went with haste and found Mary and Joseph, and the child lying in the manger. When they saw this, they made known what had been told them about this child; and all who heard

it were amazed at what the shepherds told them.
But Mary treasured all these words and pondered
them in her heart. The shepherds returned, glori-
fying and praising God for all they had heard and
seen, as it had been told them. — Luke 2:4-20

Divinity into the darkness. Miracle into the mundane. Sacred into the stable. Jesus was born. This was one of the holiest of all moments. The calendar still marks this moment. Every time we write the year, we proclaim, "Jesus is born! Holy, Holy, Holy!"

Joseph and Mary were ordinary. So ordinary were they that the Bible was clear that they came from Nazareth — a no-name northern town, stripped of significance due to patriarchal history. If this weren't ordinary enough, the birth took place on the premises of an ordinary inn. And worse! Not in the inn, but out of the inn, in the stable with animals.

Still, it was a Holy Moment. It was so holy that the hosts of heaven gathered around Bethlehem to watch. They didn't just watch; one angel had to share the Good News. Speaking to nearby shepherds, this angel said: "I am bringing you good news of great joy for all the people: to you is born this day in the city of David a Savior, who is the Messiah, the Lord."

The other angels, recognizing the holiness of this moment, joined in: "Glory to God in the highest heaven, and on earth peace among those whom he favors!"

Mary recognized this Holy Moment as she pondered and treasured in her heart all these miraculous happenings.

Could there ever be a more contrasting juxtapositioning of events than God in a manger? Perhaps God on a Cross.

Do you ever wonder if the Lord planned the entrance of Jesus Christ into the world in the most ordinary of ways so that the ordinary is sanctified? So that your life is sanctified by the presence of the Lord?

In the seventeenth century, a monk by the name of Brother Lawrence wrote a classic book titled *The Practice of the Presence of God*. Brother Lawrence found the presence of God most, not in the inner and quiet introspection of meditation and prayer, but in the outward, clamoring busyness of ordinary daily life. What perception!

I wonder how much of God's presence and activity we today miss because we are looking in the extraordinary and not the ordinary?

Questions
1. Share a time when you noticed a holy intrusion into a profoundly common setting.

2. When was the last time you seriously *pondered* the holiness of God in Jesus Christ?

3. How will you *practice the presence of God*, like Brother Lawrence, in a more intentional manner?

Prayer
God, the Father of our Lord and Savior Jesus Christ, thank You for interrupting our secular world with a reminder of Your sacred promises and intentions. Thank You for Jesus Christ, Your Son, our Redeemer. Prompt us to ponder the presence of Christ among us. Amen.

Chapter 6
Simeon At The Temple

*Now there was a man in Jerusalem whose name
was Simeon; this man was righteous and devout,
looking forward to the consolation of Israel, and
the Holy Spirit rested on him. It had been revealed
to him by the Holy Spirit that he would not see
death before he had seen the Lord's Messiah.
Guided by the Spirit, Simeon came into the temple;
and when the parents brought in the child Jesus,
to do for him what was customary under the law,
Simeon took him in his arms and praised God,
saying, "Master, now You are dismissing Your servant in peace, according to Your Word; for my eyes
have seen Your salvation, which You have prepared
in the presence of all peoples, a light for revelation to the Gentiles and for glory to Your people
Israel." And the child's father and mother were
amazed at what was being said about him. Then
Simeon blessed them and said to his mother Mary,
"This child is destined for the falling and the rising of many in Israel, and to be a sign that will be
opposed so that the inner thoughts of many will be
revealed — and a sword will pierce your own soul
too."*   — Luke 2:25-35

Have you ever felt so content, so fulfilled, and so at peace that
you wished that the Lord would take you *home*? If so, you have
experienced a Holy Moment similar to the one Simeon and Anna
experienced at the temple when Joseph and Mary brought little
eight-day-old Jesus to the temple for dedication, as was the custom
in that day.

Simeon was an old man, but a very righteous and holy man.
The Holy Spirit had revealed to him that he would not die until he

saw the Messiah. Amidst all eight-day old babies brought to the temple day after day, month after month, year after year, what enabled Simeon to recognize Jesus as the Messiah? Don't all babies look alike?

Something stood out in Jesus. Perhaps it was Jesus' countenance. Perhaps it was the same Holy Spirit who had told Simeon that Jesus was coming who also pointed out Jesus as Joseph and Mary carried baby Jesus into the temple.

Whatever it was, Simeon knew it was Jesus. What peace! What contentment! What fulfillment! What a Holy Moment! Simeon was now satisfied. Simeon, expressing this total serenity, prayed, "Now, Lord, let your servant depart (die!) in peace. Your Word has been fulfilled."

Notice what gives such peace! The fulfillment of God's Word among us! Let us take a lesson from Simeon and wait on the Lord, be alert and responsive to the promptings of the Holy Spirit, and then to call attention boldly to the fulfillment of God's promises among us as they are revealed day by day until we, like Simeon, depart in peace.

Questions

1. Have you ever waited and prayed a long time for something and then finally experienced the fulfillment of those hopes and dreams? What was it like? How did you feel?

2. When was the last time you felt so fulfilled and at peace that Simeon's prayer could have been yours? *Lord, now let your servant (me!) depart in peace....*

3. Is it realistic to expect such peace to be continual in a person's life?

Prayer

God, Master, Redeemer, Lord, grant us peace as Your Word is fulfilled day by day in our lives. Let our eyes see Your salvation in the person of Jesus Christ and in the written Word You have given to us in the Bible, which You have prepared in the presence of all peoples. Lord, let Your Son and Your Word be lights for revelation to all people and for glory to Your Name and to Your coming Kingdom, through Jesus Christ. Amen.

Chapter 7
The Transfiguration

Six days later, Jesus took with him Peter and James and his brother John and led them up a high mountain, by themselves. And he was transfigured before them, and his face shone like the sun, and his clothes became dazzling white. Suddenly there appeared to them Moses and Elijah, talking with him. Then Peter said to Jesus, "Lord, it is good for us to be here; if you wish, I will make three dwellings here, one for you, one for Moses, and one for Elijah." While he was still speaking, suddenly a bright cloud overshadowed them, and from the cloud a voice said, "This is my Son, the Beloved; with him I am well pleased; listen to him!" When the disciples heard this, they fell to the ground and were overcome by fear. But Jesus came and touched them, saying, "Get up and do not be afraid." And when they looked up, they saw no one except Jesus himself alone. — Matthew 17:1-8

Why can't certain things last forever! Some experiences are so good and so holy that it seems to us that God might want to hold that moment forever! After all, it would be a Holy Moment we would be enjoying. It's not like we are asking for a perpetual birthday party, or an endless vacation! We would love the Holy Moment of events like the Transfiguration to last forever. But the Lord knows better. He moves time along — and with time he moves us along as well.

Peter, James, and John (the three privileged disciples who accompanied Jesus on other special assignments such as keeping watch for Jesus as he prayed in the Garden of Gethsemane) followed Jesus up a mountain. Once isolated from the clamor of the crowds and the attacks by the religious power-structures, something very holy happened. Jesus was transfigured before them. Jesus' face shone like the sun; even his clothes became dazzlingly white. As if that were not enough, suddenly two of the greatest Old Testament prophets, Moses and Elijah, appeared with Jesus in this Holy Moment of heavenly revelation.

Let's not be too hard on Peter. He spoke what James and John were probably thinking (and what you and I would also be thinking at that moment). *This is good, Lord. We like this. This is a far cry better than fighting the crowds down in the valley. Let's make this moment and this mountain the command post for the Kingdom! If you wish, Lord, I will make three houses, one for you, one for Moses, and one for Elijah, and we can just stay up here and coordinate the Kingdom from here!*

Once in a while two Holy Moments occur in rapid succession. Such happened here. Just at the end of the miracle of the Transfiguration, a cloud overshadowed them and God's voice boomed from Heaven, "This is my Son, the Beloved; with him I am well pleased; listen to him!"

Peter, James, and John fell prostrate to the ground. Perhaps they were thinking thoughts that have filled my mind when I have put forth my plans without first listening to Jesus!

Have you ever noticed what happened next? *When they looked up, they saw no one except Jesus.* It's not that Moses and Elijah disappeared and it's not that the view from the mountain top was obscured. Rather, after the Holy Moments of the Transfiguration and God's Word spoken from the clouds, they now saw Jesus more clearly. That often happens after Holy Moments!

Questions

1. When was the last time you got so excited about some Christian ministry program that you set out to accomplish it without first consulting with (praying to) the Lord?

2. When was the last time God's Word corrected your thought on a matter?

3. When was the last time God led you back to the valley to labor among God's people rather than to remain forever in a prayer closet or spiritual retreat?

Prayer

Dear Lord, we praise and thank You that You know best what we need and what our world needs. Please give us such glimpses of Your coming Kingdom and Holiness that we are fed and strengthened to listen to and obey Your Word as we labor and witness in the valleys of life. One more thing, Lord: please keep our eyes fixed on You. Amen.

Chapter 8
The Lord's Last Supper

For I received from the Lord what I also handed on to you, that the Lord Jesus on the night when he was betrayed took a loaf of bread, and when he had given thanks, he broke it and said, "This is my body that is for you. Do this in remembrance of me." In the same way he took the cup also, after supper, saying, "This cup is the new covenant in my blood. Do this, as often as you drink it, in remembrance of me." For as often as you eat this bread and drink the cup, you proclaim the Lord's death until he comes. — 1 Corinthians 11:23-26

The Apostle Paul wrote the fourth account of the Last Supper in the New Testament. There are several noteworthy items in this account that we would do well to study.

First, note that the Lord through Paul expresses an apostolic nature to the Lord's Supper, "For I received from the Lord what I also handed on to you." The implication? Each generation, each believing community, and each Christian are part of the passing on and evangelical expansion of God's plan of salvation and coming Kingdom.

"This is my body that is for you ... This cup is the new covenant in my blood." These words are holy words. These words announce a Holy Moment every time they are spoken over the bread and cup in the midst of believers. We may not fully understand what is happening in this Holy Moment, such as how Jesus Christ is present in, with, and under the bread and the wine, but we do know that we are commanded by our Lord to observe this sacramental meal often. The word "often" is used twice in two sentences.

Have you noticed the last sentence in the above passage? It reminds us that as often as we observe this meal we "proclaim the

Lord's death until he comes." Communion is not just personal communion between thee and me; it is a public testimony and proclamation of both the Lord's saving death on the Cross and Christ's second coming. The Holy Moment that occurs at the celebration of the Lord's Supper has a far greater audience than many Christians realize.

Questions
1. What do you think of when you receive the Lord's Supper?

2. What do you think is going on in the hearts and lives of those who are present during Communion but who do not receive the elements? Is a saving message still being proclaimed and heard?

3. How often should the Lord's Supper be part of Christian worship?

4. Talk about the many messages and gifts *in* the Lord's Supper.

Prayer
Thank you, Lord Jesus, for loving us so much that you died in our place, paying the penalty for our sins and offering us new life as we receive you into our lives. Give us a hunger for your Word. Never let our thirst for you be quenched. Come, Lord Jesus. Amen.

Chapter 9
Noon — 3 p.m. On Good Friday

*From noon on, darkness came over the whole land
until three in the afternoon. And about three o'clock
Jesus cried with a loud voice, "Eli, Eli, lema
sabachthani?" that is, "My God, my God, why
have you forsaken me?" When some of the bystand-
ers heard it, they said, "This man is calling for
Elijah." At once one of them ran and got a sponge,
filled it with sour wine, put it on a stick, and gave
it to him to drink. But the others said, "Wait, let us
see whether Elijah will come to save him." Then
Jesus cried again with a loud voice and breathed
his last. At that moment the curtain of the temple
was torn in two, from top to bottom. The earth
shook, and the rocks were split.*
— Matthew 27:45-51

The holiest of all moments occurred at about 3 p.m. on the
Friday Jesus was crucified on a Cross effecting an offer of forgiveness and salvation to all people.

The drama on Golgotha was building. All but one of the disciples had fled. Jesus' mother and a few of his women followers
were at the foot of the Cross. The Roman soldiers were dividing
the spoils from another crucifixion. The Pharisees and Scribes were
thinking they had gotten rid of a troublemaker.

Suddenly, darkness overshadowed them. The earth shook so
hard that rocks were split. And it was not just a localized Holy
Moment. What did those making preparation in the temple on the
day before the Sabbath think when suddenly the temple curtain
ripped in two, from top to bottom?

The people who witnessed this Holy Moment were not the ones
who most understood it. The real participants and spectators in this
drama were spiritual. God the Father saw His own and only Son

dying for a lost world. The demonic forces of this world grimaced as they saw a payment made that at one and the same time satisfied perfect divine justice and dealt a deadly blow to their grasp and control of the world.

It was a Holy Moment that was beyond our comprehension. Something huge happened. Something unique and unrepeatable happened that altered the course of human history. Cluelessly, the world soon began marking time by dating future years in reference to the birth date of Jesus Christ who was crucified. Generation after generation continues to look back at that Holy Moment as the fulcrum of history and a watershed event faced by every human being.

Questions

1. What actually happened in Heaven and on earth at the very moment Jesus died?

2. Why did the temple curtain tear from top to bottom, not bottom to top?

3. Why did Jesus say he felt "forsaken" by his Heavenly Father?

4. When was the last time you were around something BIG that happened and didn't realize the importance of the event until later?

Prayer

Almighty God, a divine drama occurred on the Cross of Calvary. It was a Holy Moment fully understood only by Your Son Jesus hanging on the Cross and You Who, as our Heavenly Father, were reconciling the world's debt by Jesus' blood. As Your children who are now even filled with Your Holy Spirit, we still do not fully comprehend the Crucifixion — yet there will never be a holier moment, ever! Thank you, Jesus. Amen.

Chapter 10
Easter Morning

After the sabbath, as the first day of the week was dawning, Mary Magdalene and the other Mary went to see the tomb. And suddenly there was a great earthquake; for an angel of the Lord, descending from heaven, came and rolled back the stone and sat on it. His appearance was like lightning, and his clothing white as snow. For fear of him the guards shook and became like dead men. But the angel said to the women, "Do not be afraid; I know that you are looking for Jesus who was crucified. He is not here; for he has been raised, as he said. Come, see the place where he lay. Then go quickly and tell his disciples, 'He has been raised from the dead, and indeed he is going ahead of you to Galilee; there you will see him.' This is my message for you." So they left the tomb quickly with fear and great joy, and ran to tell his disciples. — Matthew 28:1-8

Have you ever been interrupted with joy in the midst of your grief? What you thought was a tragedy turned out to be an opportunity? What you thought was a downfall turned out to be a windfall?

The two Marys on Easter morning went to the tomb out of duty and respect for the dead — their dead leader, named Jesus. They were sad, grief-stricken, disappointed, and just plain heartbroken; they loved Jesus.

It wasn't enough to announce to these ladies that Jesus was alive. Our Heavenly Father added some drama to punctuate this Holy Moment: an earthquake, an angel, a stone rolled away, and a theophany of an angel.

The women listened, took it all in, and then quickly ran to tell the disciples the great news.

How quickly moods can change! Over the years, I have learned that there is a certain undulation to life. There will be troughs of sadness and despair; but there will also be peaks and mountaintop experiences. Therefore, I have learned to hope in the midst of despair, and to temper my tendency toward overexuberance in the midst of joy. Most of all, I have learned that what matters most is not the peaks or valleys along life's journeys, but rather keeping my eyes fixed on Jesus along the way. When I do this, then like the Apostle Paul, I find that "I can be content in all circumstances" (1 Timothy 4:11-12).

Questions
1. Share a time in your life when you almost gave up.

2. What was it that enabled you to move on from your despair? After all, you are here today!

3. How easy it is to jump to wrong conclusions! How easy it is to give up! Discuss whether or not the women and the other disciples were weak in faith by assuming Jesus' death on that first Easter morning.

4. When has the Lord "shaken your world" with the Holy Moment of Good News, teaching you to trust him?

Prayer
Dear Living Lord, may we never give up on you or your promises! We may give up on ourselves, our world, others, but teach us, by surprising us with your grace and power, never to give up on you! May we run today and tell others this important message, in Jesus' Name! Amen.

Chapter 11
Easter Evening

When it was evening on that day, the first day of the week, and the doors of the house where the disciples had met were locked for fear of the Jews, Jesus came and stood among them and said, "Peace be with you." After he said this, he showed them his hands and his side. Then the disciples rejoiced when they saw the Lord. Jesus said to them again, "Peace be with you. As the Father has sent me, so I send you." When he had said this, he breathed on them and said to them, "Receive the Holy Spirit. If you forgive the sins of any, they are forgiven them; if you retain the sins of any, they are retained." But Thomas (who was called the Twin), one of the twelve, was not with them when Jesus came. So the other disciples told him, "We have seen the Lord." But he said to them, "Unless I see the mark of the nails in his hands, and put my finger in the mark of the nails and my hand in his side, I will not believe." A week later his disciples were again in the house, and Thomas was with them. Although the doors were shut, Jesus came and stood among them and said, "Peace be with you." Then he said to Thomas, "Put your finger here and see my hands. Reach out your hand and put it in my side. Do not doubt but believe." Thomas answered him, "My Lord and my God!"
— John 20:19-28

Holy Moments often occur in the midst of other moments. Even though the women had told them that Jesus had been raised, and even though the Lord had already appeared to Peter, the disciples were paralyzed in their fear. Survival instincts had taken over their lives! Fearing a fate similar to that which occurred to their Lord, they holed up like scared animals in their den.

The holiness of both of these Holy Moments which occurred on the first two Sundays after Jesus' resurrection was dramatized by the magnitude of the fear that the disciples were feeling just prior to these Holy Moments. The disciples' courage had waned during the previous two weeks. The Bible tells us that "all the disciples deserted Jesus and fled" (Matthew 26:56) when Jesus was arrested. Even at the foot of the Cross, only the beloved disciple, John, hung around long enough to see Jesus hang on the Cross. It was now a week and three days later. One can only imagine the conversation occurring in the upper room: "And we had hoped he was the one!" (Luke 24:21). "Now what are we going to do? I hope Dad hasn't sold the extra boats!" Or, more probably, "I wonder if they [the Scribes and Pharisees] know where we are! And I wonder if they will do the same thing to us!"

Into this cacophony of dashed dreams and fears, Jesus suddenly appeared and brought peace. Indeed, three times he spoke the words, "Peace be with you." Jesus even met Thomas *where Thomas was* — in his doubts. Thomas needed proof; Jesus gave proof. Thomas believed, "My Lord and my God."

In this Holy Moment, Thomas' doubts were transformed to deep belief. Perhaps this experience made Thomas a stronger believer in his later years because Thomas no longer let his doubts cloud the absolute certitude of Christ's reality and power!

Questions

1. Have you ever been so afraid of something or someone that you isolated yourself?

2. How do you think Thomas felt after being so sure of his doubts only to have Jesus *prove* to Thomas that he, indeed, had risen from the dead?

3. Share a time when some "Good News" brought peace to your life.

4. How does it feel to admit that you were wrong — that your doubts about something were ill-founded?

5. How can this Holy Moment for Thomas strengthen you in your own struggles with doubts in the Christian life?

Prayer

Almighty God, Gracious Lord, Living Savior, thank you for revealing yourself to us in ways that dispel our doubts. Please show us the foolishness of doubting you and your Holy Word; instead, Lord, help us, like Thomas to exclaim, "My Lord and my God!" as you break into our world and doubts again and again and again. In Holy Moment after Holy Moment, bring us peace through Jesus Christ. Amen.

Chapter 12
The Ordinary

Now when they saw the boldness of Peter and John and realized that they were uneducated and ordinary men, they (the rulers, elders, and scribes) were amazed and recognized them as companions of Jesus. When they saw the man who had been cured standing beside them, they had nothing to say in opposition. So they ordered them to leave the council while they discussed the matter with one another. They said, "What will we do with them? For it is obvious to all who live in Jerusalem that a notable sign has been done through them; we cannot deny it. But to keep it from spreading further among the people, let us warn them to speak no more to anyone in this name." So they called them and ordered them not to speak or teach at all in the name of Jesus. But Peter and John answered them, "Whether it is right in God's sight to listen to you rather than to God, you must judge; for we cannot keep from speaking about what we have seen and heard." — Acts 4:13-20

Oh, how I love these verses! *Ordinary people!* That's all the Lord wants us to be! Ordinary people who love him so much that they *cannot keep from speaking* about him — even if it means persecution!

Our Lord is so powerful that he can take ordinary people, infuse them with his Holy Word and gospel message, and turn them into powerful instruments, fully accomplishing his will, not by any virtue of their own, but solely by the power of his Name!

Isn't this how sacraments work? Ordinary elements like water, bread, and wine combine with God's Holy Word and miracles occur! It is not because the water, bread, or wine are good in and of themselves or effective by themselves; rather, sacraments *work* because Christ promised to *work* through them (some theologians have coined the terms, *in, with,* and *under,* to describe how God's grace is present in the sacraments).

I also love this passage because it boldly names the *Name of Jesus.* How often we beat around the bush when it comes to sharing the gospel. How often our timidity parades as politeness. For Peter and John, they couldn't help but name the Name. Have you ever noticed that the authorities who detained Peter and John didn't care if they preached, or did miracles, or did anything else as long at they no longer did so *in his Name*? There is power in the Name of Jesus! Name it! Claim it! Frame it in your heart! Jesus Christ is your Lord and Savior! Because of what he has done for us, how can we keep quiet? Indeed, even if we remain silent, the very stones will cry out (Luke 19:40)! I don't know about you, but I don't want the stones out-witnessing me!

Questions

1. When was the last time you felt very *ordinary*? Does this passage help you see that being *ordinary* people who love Jesus is just fine?

2. Notice that when Peter and John spoke, even though they were *ordinary* people, the rulers, leaders, and scribes *recognized* that they were *companions of Jesus* — what great company! Would that others would so recognize us! Do people recognize you as a *companion of Jesus*?

3. Do you boldly *name the Name* of Jesus Christ frequently in your daily conversation? Or are you *politically correct* and refrain from using a Savior-specific name in favor of broad generalities like "God" or "higher power"?

4. Do you believe that Christ can use you *sacramentally*? That is, do you believe that God can take the ordinary efforts, witness,

works, deeds, teaching, and love that you offer verbally in his Name and then add his grace and produce miracles?

Prayer

Almighty God, Father of our Lord and Savior Jesus Christ, You are extraordinary; we are ordinary! You have entered our life through the supernatural birth of Jesus Christ in human form. You have redeemed the unrighteous; You have sanctified the sinful; You have made the ordinary extraordinary; and You have made the natural supernatural. All this You have done by means of Your Son, Jesus Christ, and his death on the Cross for us. Lord, fill us to overflowing with Your Holy Spirit and with a love for You that cannot be contained within our mortal bodies! We ask this as we desire to do everything in our lives — in the Name of Jesus Christ. Amen!

Chapter 13
On A Road To Damascus

Meanwhile Saul, still breathing threats and mur-
der against the disciples of the Lord, went to the
high priest and asked him for letters to the syna-
gogues at Damascus, so that if he found any who
belonged to the Way, men or women, he might bring
them bound to Jerusalem. Now as he was going
along and approaching Damascus, suddenly a
light from heaven flashed around him. He fell to
the ground and heard a voice saying to him, "Saul,
Saul, why do you persecute me?" He asked, "Who
are you, Lord?" The reply came, "I am Jesus,
whom you are persecuting. But get up and enter
the city, and you will be told what you are to do."
                                    — Acts 9:1-6

Saul, the greatest persecutor of the early church, later became
known as Paul, the greatest missionary of the early church. How
did this happen? By means of a Holy Moment! Saul was on his
way to Damascus to capture and persecute more Christians. How
seriously did Saul persecute Christians? Acts 22:4 tells us that he
persecuted Christians *up to the point of death.* Saul was feared by
Christians.

If ever there were an unlikely candidate to become a propo-
nent of Christianity, it was Saul! "Bingo," the Lord said, "Here is
the one I will use." You see, God would rather use us in our areas of
weakness so that the praise and glory would go to Him. If the Lord
were regularly to use us in our fields of strength, you and I, being
human, would quickly, with of course an abundant serving of false
humility, usurp the Lord for credit. Look back over biblical history
and witness the unlikely candidates the Lord conscripted into His
service so that there would be no question as to where the praise

and glory should go: Moses was slow of speech, David was a shepherd boy, James and John were known as sons of thunder, and Mary Magdalene had a past. Yet, each of these people played powerful roles in His-story — by His grace.

Saul got a new life. It was as if he were born again. Hence, the new name, Paul. The first thing Paul did was to obey Jesus and go into the city to which he was directed. After that first step, many other steps followed — three, perhaps four, missionary journeys, shipwrecks, beatings, persecution, imprisonment, and hunger. All this happened because of a Holy Moment which changed the direction of Paul's life — eternally.

Questions

1. The letters of Ephesians and 1 Peter frequently use the phrase, "once you were ... but now you are ..." to describe the life-changing transformation that the Lord works in the lives of those who accept Holy Moments. Can you share how a Holy Moment in your life transformed you in a "once-you-were ... but-now-you-are ..." manner?

2. When did the Lord call you to do something that was outside of your gift-set, comfort-range, or reputation? Did you obey faithfully? How successful was your obedience?

3. Have people around you, such as friends, family, or co-workers, noticed a change in you due to a Holy Moment encounter that you have had with Jesus Christ?

Prayer

God Almighty, Creator, Redeemer, and Sustainer, how we praise and thank You for Your power and presence in our lives and world! How we praise and thank You for working among us and within us in unlikely ways! Let us never give up hope in You, Lord. Let us grow in our expectation and dependence upon You to call us, equip us, and use us in ways that we cannot imagine, but in ways that we know You are able! Thank you, Father, for Your work in Paul's life. Help us, Lord, to respond to our own holy-moment-Damascus-Road-experiences in ways that are as faithful and obedient as Paul's response. And then, Lord, use us as Your instruments, for Jesus' sake and in his Name. Amen.

Chapter 14
By An Ethiopian's Chariot

Then an angel of the Lord said to Philip, "Get up and go toward the south to the road that goes down from Jerusalem to Gaza." (This is a wilderness road.) So he got up and went. Now there was an Ethiopian eunuch, a court official of Candace, queen of the Ethiopians, in charge of her entire treasury. He had come to Jerusalem to worship and was returning home; seated in his chariot, he was reading the prophet Isaiah. Then the Spirit said to Philip, "Go over to this chariot and join it." So Philip ran up to it and heard him reading the prophet Isaiah. He asked, "Do you understand what you are reading?" He replied, "How can I, unless someone guides me?" And he invited Philip to get in and sit beside him. Now the passage of the scripture that he was reading was this: "Like a sheep he was led to the slaughter, and like a lamb silent before its shearer, so he does not open his mouth. In his humiliation justice was denied him. Who can describe his generation? For his life is taken away from the earth." The eunuch asked Philip, "About whom, may I ask you, does the prophet say this, about himself or about someone else?" Then Philip began to speak, and starting with this scripture, he proclaimed to him the good news about Jesus. As they were going along the road, they came to some water; and the eunuch said, "Look, here is water! What is to prevent me from being baptized?" He commanded the chariot to stop, and both of them, Philip and the eunuch, went down into the water, and Philip baptized him.
— Acts 8:26-38

Philip was one of the seven deacons appointed, in Acts 6, to "serve" the church and to ensure that the preaching of the gospel was not overlooked. Philip, indeed, did serve. What I like best about this Philip, the Deacon, is his availability. The Lord, you see, is not so much interested in our abilities; the Lord equips us with the skills and abilities we need for the tasks to which He calls us. The Lord is most interested in and affected by our availability — our willingness to serve when and how the Lord desires.

Picture Philip traveling along the wilderness road from Jerusalem to Gaza. At the same time, an Ethiopian official was traveling this same road. Since he was a high ranking official, this man was traveling in a chariot. Unbeknownst to Philip, the official was reading from the scroll of Isaiah. The moment was right and ripe. The Lord called upon Philip to become available suddenly and immediately to this inquisitive soul reading God's Word. Philip hastened to the chariot and then one's imagination takes over. Did he run along side and try to strike up a conversation by asking, "Hey there! What are you reading? Do you understand it? Can I be of any service?" The moment was right; the moment was holy — prepared and orchestrated by the Lord. The Ethiopian official opened his soul; Philip offered his availability to the Lord. God's Word did the work of introducing this man to Jesus. Nothing prevented this Ethiopian from being baptized. And a soul was saved.

Questions
1. How available have you been in the past to the Lord for His special service projects?

2. Have you even "been at just the right place at the right time" for some purpose of the Lord? Did you recognize it as a Holy Moment that invited your "availability"?

3. How ready are you to lead a person to a saving relationship with Jesus Christ? Do you have a few key Bible passages (such as Jeremiah 29:13; John 3:16; Romans 3:23, 4:25, 10:9,

Galatians 2:20; Revelation 3:20) memorized? Do you "look for" or "shy away from" such opportunities?

4. Read and discuss 1 Peter 3:15. How ready are you?

Prayer

Great God of the Universe and Savior of my soul, how we praise and thank You that You are in control — not only of history and the ultimate direction of Your creation, but also of the encounters and opportunities that occur every day. Please, Lord, help us to "be ready" to give a gentle and faithful witness and testimony to whomever You place in our path today, in Jesus' Name. Amen.

Chapter 15
Silence

When the Lamb opened the seventh seal, there was
silence in heaven for about half an hour.
— Revelation 8:1

Holy, Holy, Holy! In the book of Revelation, the opening of the
Seven Seals is the beginning of the Beginning of Christ's return
and reign! Earlier in Revelation, chapter 4, in a vision of the throne
of Heaven, the four living creatures around the throne day and night
announce the holiness of the Lord God Almighty with the opening
words of this paragraph. Four chapters later, the silence equally
announces the holiness, omniscience, sovereignty, power, majesty,
and glory of the Lamb of God, Jesus Christ!

Have you ever been awestruck by something? Have you ever
had to stand stupefied in the presence of the wonder of something
or someone? Sometimes words fail and it is not only acceptable,
but very proper, just to behold an event, a kindness, a person, a
beauty. After all, words could not capture the wonder, the magnifi-
cence, and the holiness of the moment.

I've heard it said that the first word to be uttered in Heaven
will be, "Oh!" — as in "Now I understand" or "Now I see" (as in
face to face, 1 Corinthians 13:12). Perhaps our first thirty minutes
in Heaven will be filled with no words at all, just awestruck silence
as we gaze upon the Lamb upon the throne.

Questions
1. What do you think Heaven will be like?

2. Share a time when you were so awestruck by some experi-
    ence, person, or event that no human words could express your
    feelings or thoughts.

4. Describe the most "holy" event or moment you've ever experienced.

Prayer

Heavenly King, Lord God Almighty, how holy and majestic is Your Name! How humbly I come before You even now in my prayers! How much more humble will I feel when I some day see You face to face and behold Your beauty, glory, and splendor! Still my anxieties, Lord; calm my heart; silence my voice; let me simply worship and adore You, not just when You come in Your glory, but even in this very Holy Moment of intimate communication of prayer through Your Son, the Lamb of God, through whom I pray. Amen.

Holy
Moments
In
This Life

Chapter 16
Christmas Eve —
Late And At Home

*"Peace I leave with you; my peace I give to you. I
do not give to you as the world gives. Do not let
your hearts be troubled, and do not let them be
afraid."* — John 14:27

One of my holiest moments experienced breaks into my life
once a year. It occurs in the living room of our house, while seated
on a sofa with my wife, at about 1:30 a.m. on Christmas morning.

Let me please first set the scene. The eight to ten hours prior to
this Holy Moment are important. Indeed, without these hours setting the scene, there would be no Holy Moment to be experienced.
The eight to ten hours before the Holy Moment occur on Christmas
Eve; the Holy Moment itself takes place early Christmas morning.

The eight to ten hours prior to the Holy Moment are filled with
Christmas worship, carols, poinsettias, luminaries, hundreds of
people, and choirs. Though tiring, the long day has been holy in
itself. Celebrating the birth and presence of Jesus Christ is one of
the most joyous times of the entire year.

After the last Christmas Eve candlelight service, the worshipers slowly disperse into the dark night with hearts aglow. Suddenly,
"Silent Night, Holy Night" sets in at the church. I am alone in the
church. I make the rounds turning off lights, unplugging Christmas trees, locking doors, and picking up personal items left by
worshipers. I walk to my car, get in, and drive home — choosing to
sing Christmas carols to myself rather than listen to the radio. The
streets are bare. The air is cool. There seems to be Holiness draped
over the world that is unique to Christmas Eve. I'm tired. My feet
are sore. My back is tired. I know that I will have to get out of bed
in just a few hours to open Christmas presents with my family. But

I am in no hurry to go to bed. Indeed, I know that I am on my way to experiencing one of the holiest moments of the year.

I arrive home. Lights are still on. My wife Cindy is waiting up for me. The Christmas tree lights are still on. The fire is out in the fireplace, but I can still smell the glowing burnt embers. Cindy knows that a Holy Moment is about to occur. We don't have to discuss or plan for the Holy Moment. We meet in the kitchen, pour glasses of eggnog, and then together walk to the living room where we sit down together on the love seat.

The Holy Moment arrives. Not magically, just miraculously. Jesus is present with us. Time stops. Contentment and peace fill and surround us. Cindy asks how the worship services were. We look at the tree filled with ornaments. We both are overwhelmed with feelings of gratitude. Oh, not that all of the years have been easy! Some of the years included cancer, deaths of loved ones, illnesses, and trials. But these events and the memories of these events just make the moment holier.

The Holy Moment lasts about thirty minutes. Then, it's bed time. Christmas morning and the children at the foot of our bed are only a few hours away. Cindy and I, having shared a Holy Moment, know that time marches on — but we also know that "Immanuel," God is with us!

Questions

1. When is the holiest moment of your annual Christmas celebration?

2. Do you have a tradition or two in your family that are as holy and meaningful as this tradition in our family? Please share such traditions. If you do not have one, please plan one.

3. Do you think that the Lord still "visits" the earth in a special spiritual way on Christmas Eve — making it a "holy night" that somehow touches even the most resistant of souls?

Prayer

Almighty God, Father of our Lord and Savior Jesus Christ, thank You for not giving up on Your fallen and lost Creation! Thank You for coming into our world through Your only Son, Jesus Christ, at Bethlehem for the purpose of redeeming us — of buying us back through the payment of Your Son's life given on a Cross for the sins of a fallen world. Only through Your presence and grace can any holiness enter our world. Please, Lord, make us sensitive to Your presence. You are still with us! Immanuel! Amen!

Chapter 17
5:15 a.m.

In the morning, while it was still very dark, he got up and went out to a deserted place, and there he prayed. — Mark 1:35

And all the people would get up early in the morning to listen to him in the temple. — Luke 21:38

I'm not a morning person. This Holy Moment habit of getting up early and beginning my day with devotions happened out of necessity rather than choice. When else can a person find solitude, quiet, and time for Bible reading and prayer? Come sun-up, the world is up, the children need help, the television's on, and the rush to get ready for school and work is on! That's why 5:15 a.m. is a Holy Moment I cherish every day.

Rather than escape to a lonely isolated place up on a mountain or in a garden, my holy retreat is the dining room table. There, with my Bible, my devotional booklet, my prayer list, and the directory of our church, I meet the Lord in a holy morning meeting. Let me please share the format of this daily routine.

- I begin with the Bible — reading the passage assigned by a devotional booklet I use. Occasionally, I end up reading beyond the assigned reading, or I get sidetracked by the Living Word as it speaks anew to me. But, most of the time, I finish the scripture passage and then read the devotional passage.

- Second, I pray through my prayer list. This is a list that I print out on Monday morning of every week and then add to throughout the week. The list contains names of my family members, people known to us who are ill, members of our church family with needs, extended family, missionaries, praise-petitions, requests, the future husband and wife of our children should they get married, the mission of Christ's Church (locally and globally), and finally three people — my mentor (a "Paul"), someone I am mentoring (a "Timothy"), and a training partner (a "Barnabas"). Every week, I identify specific names in the blank lines of these three important people in my Christian walk.

- Third, I read my mission statement — which is always printed on my prayer list. My personal mission statement is as follows. *Created by God, lost through sin, redeemed by Christ, and renewed by the Holy Spirit, I strive to be a faithful steward of all that the Lord has entrusted to my care, striving to reach the most number of people most effectively for Jesus Christ.*
- Fourth and finally, I open our church's membership directory to the page number which corresponds to the date of the present month. I then pray for each person and family on the page. This enables me to pray for, by name, each and every person in our congregation every month.
- Oh, yes — coffee is also a part of this morning meeting!

Questions:

1. Do you have a holy time and holy place when and where you "meet the Lord" on a daily basis? Describe such a time and place.

2. How can a daily Holy Moment with the Lord be strengthening?

3. Commit to making a weekly prayer list. Include immediate family, those with particular needs (physical, emotional, spiritual), praise as well as petition, concerns, and repentance.

Prayer
Gracious Lord, You invite us to pray. Even the disciples only asked Your Son to teach them one thing — and that was to pray. Lord, please teach us to pray. Please give us a hunger for Your Word.

Please let us never think that we are too busy to set aside daily Sabbath time during which we seek Your face, read Your Word, and listen to You in prayer — all through the merit and grace of Your Son, Jesus Christ, our Lord. Amen.

Chapter 18
At The Communion Rail

Then Jesus went about all the cities and villages,
teaching in their synagogues, and proclaiming the
good news of the kingdom, and curing every dis-
ease and every sickness. When he saw the crowds,
he had compassion for them, because they were
harassed and helpless, like sheep without a shep-
herd. — Matthew 9:35-36

While they were eating, Jesus took a loaf of bread,
and after blessing it he broke it, gave it to the dis-
ciples, and said, "Take, eat; this is my body." Then
he took a cup, and after giving thanks he gave it to
them, saying, "Drink from it, all of you; for this is
my blood of the covenant, which is poured out for
many for the forgiveness of sins."
— Matthew 26:26-28

I love this Holy Moment! It gives me a glimpse of people through the eyes of Christ. At least, that is what seems to be occurring every time this Holy Moment occurs.

There are many Holy Moments during a Holy Communion service. The time of Confession and Absolution is holy as the miracle of forgiveness occurs at the beginning of worship. The reading of God's Word is holy as words of immortality are spoken by mortals to mortals in the presence of the Immortal! And, of course, the consecration of the bread and wine or grape juice is holy as during this time, we "proclaim the Lord's death until he comes."

But, for me, one of the Holiest Moments is during the distribution of communion. The invitation is given. In our church, people come forward to the altar rail to receive the bread and the wine or juice. They kneel. Some people smile. Some cry. Some tremble. Some even "raise the glass" as if to say, "Salut!" (This actually isn't that untheological! "Salut" of course means health and in the ancient liturgy of the church, the preface to Holy Communion included this phrase, "It is meet, right, and salutary that at all times and in all places it is right to give praise and thanks to You, Almighty God, Father of our Lord Jesus Christ....")

The holiest part of distribution for me is when I see person after person kneeling at the altar rail, receiving in the bread and the wine the assurance of forgiveness, life, and eternal salvation given and shed for each of them. I think that part of the holiness of the moment is that each person is so different, yet each person has the same desperate need of what Jesus is offering.

Please let me share a view of just a few people I see at every communion rail. First, there is the couple who have been married over 55 years; they are in church almost every week. They've been in church almost every week for the past 75 years! They are pillars; they are like Simeon and Anna in Luke 2, except they are married to each other! They have their problems, but they are rock solid when it comes to their blind trust in and love for Jesus Christ.

Next, there is the middle-aged couple — a couple that everyone else in the church thinks is fine, successful, and happy. Yet the pastor knows. This couple is in trouble — deep trouble. Marital infidelity, financial impropriety, addiction, or a combination of the above. Only one has been in for counseling so far; the other is trying to tough it out or deny the problem. One thing they both know at this moment — the Lord cares for them and the pastor prays for them. Maybe a miracle will occur.

A high school student kneels next. She has a deep and sincere faith. I think of young Timothy or young King David in the Bible when I place the wafer in her hand. As I pass on to the next person, I hear the wafer crack in two before the high school student places it in her mouth. I marvel how in every church I've ever served, some people always break the wafer as if to remind themselves that the Body of Christ was *broken* for them.

Next is a widow — alone, yet surrounded by family and the "cloud of witnesses" at the communion rail. She has tears in her eyes; yet she smiles. I cry.

Next comes someone who is difficult to love. Occasionally this person is one with whom I've had a recent disagreement, or one who just plain does not like my preaching or my ideas or my looks, or one whom I unjustly judged or offended in my humanness. We share in a holy encounter at the altar rail, linked and reconciled at one and the same time through the body and blood of Jesus Christ.

My family comes forward. They kneel. They receive from my hand the saving grace of Jesus Christ. How humbling. How this reminds me of how often I fail at being the husband and father the Lord called me to be. Yet, in this meal we are reminded how our wonderful Lord brings his saving grace through humble means — like bread and wine, and like fathers and mothers.

Questions

1. Describe the last time you received the Lord's Supper. Did you recognize the Holy Moment?

2. Have you ever helped distribute the bread or the wine? Does your church or fellowship allow or encourage lay participants in this part of the service? If so, ask if you can assist distribute communion.

3. What are your thoughts and feelings at the moment you receive Holy Communion?

4. The next time you receive Holy Communion, pray for people at the very moment they receive the bread and the wine. If you know the person, pray for concerns in his or her life. If you do not know the people, pray that they may experience in that moment a Holy Moment!

Prayer

Gracious God and Father of our Lord Jesus Christ, You are merciful, You are loving, and You desire that not one of Your children will be lost, but that everyone will come to repentance and live. In the

Holy Moment of Communion, we meet You as our Father Who so loves the world that You gave Your one and only Son so that whoever believes and receives him as Lord and Savior will never die, but will have eternal life. Through the body and blood of Christ, in Holy Communion, we are embraced by the outstretched arms of Christ and thereby welcomed home by our Heavenly Father. Amen.

Chapter 19
At The Altar Rail — Marriage

"For this reason a man will leave his father and mother and be joined to his wife, and the two will become one flesh." This is a great mystery, and I am applying it to Christ and the church.
— Ephesians 5:31-32

I think the Holiest Moment of a wedding occurs at the instant that the bride appears at the entrance to the church. Time seems to freeze. Hearts are warm. The groom, standing at the end of the aisle near the altar, gazes at the woman he is about to marry. Everybody else is also looking at the bride; there is a myriad of emotions and thoughts occurring at that Holy Moment.

The mother of the bride is crying tears of joy because her baby is grown, beautiful, and loved. Perhaps a couple tears are because of a separation that is occurring in this Holy Moment.

The father of the bride has butterflies in his stomach as he is about to walk his daughter down the aisle.

The bride is loved by everyone at the wedding; love radiates from her as she steps into the view of the congregation. All eyes are on her.

The groom loves the bride and looks affectionately at her as she approaches him.

The stage for the miracle is set. Two are about to become one. As words and promises are exchanged, the world is once again given a foretaste of *the* wedding that will occur when the bride of Christ, the Church, will be gowned in a robe washed white in the blood of the Lamb, and will approach the Groom, who is Jesus Christ. Then will the stage — the final stage — be set for a miracle — the greatest and longest lasting marriage feast ever!

Questions

1. Describe the Holy Moment of when the bride appeared in the doorway of the church at the last wedding you attended. Did you sense the holiness?

2. What does God's Word mean in Ephesians 5 when it says, "This is a great mystery, and I am applying it to Christ and the church?"

3. What can you do to rescue marriage from its current state in our culture and reverence it in the sacramental way that the Lord designed it?

Prayer

Gracious Lord, Lover of all souls, Redeemer of a lost creation, and Keeper of covenants and vows made to Your Church: How You love us! How we fail to understand the depth of love with which You love us! How faithful You are! How blessed we are! How happy we will be when we stand, by Your grace, garbed in Your righteousness, before You. Then, and only then, will we see, no longer dimly, but face to face. Then, and only then, will we finally understand — even as we have been all along fully understood and loved by Your Son, Jesus Christ, our Lord, our Savior, and our Bridegroom. Amen.

Chapter 20
Birth

For it was you who formed my inward parts; you knit me together in my mother's womb. I praise you, for I am fearfully and wonderfully made. Wonderful are your works; that I know very well. My frame was not hidden from you, when I was being made in secret, intricately woven in the depths of the earth. Your eyes beheld my unformed substance. In your book were written all the days that were formed for me, when none of them as yet existed. How weighty to me are your thoughts, O God! How vast is the sum of them!

— Psalm 139:13-17

The birth of a child is a Holy Moment — for everyone. The parents, of course, are awestruck at the unfathomable thought that they "begat" this child. The mystery of the event is often lost in the myriad tasks of taking care of the child! Yet the thought that this child is a miracle persistently surfaces above the piles of diapers, crib sheets, and baby clothes. Each of those "surfacings" is a Holy Moment when the parents recognize that once again the separation between Heaven and earth was just bridged by God's delivery of a new life.

The Holy Moment isn't just reserved for the parents. The doctors, nurses, and other medical staff, just doing their duties, are spectators of the sacred. They are the first to admit that they are not the miracle-workers producing this gift of a child. God is at work; the earth is silent as it witnesses such miracles. Even the toughest agnostics in a maternity ward withhold their caustic comments in the presence of such an obvious bridging of worlds they other times hold to be totally separated.

As the parents' perspective on time changes due to the all-consuming demands of caring for this new family member, "pondering" (like Mother Mary did so well) becomes part of parenthood. The mother ponders the delivery and how the pain of it so quickly disappeared after the delivery. The father ponders how the addition of a new family member doesn't further divide a limited amount of love a family has to share; rather, the family's love expands to embrace the newcomer without lessening the love that was shared prior to the birth. If only the economy of finance worked like the economy of divine love!

Every once in a while, even the world ponders the similarity between the groans and pains of labor, which give way to the joy and laughter of birth, and the groans and pains that often accompany the "other end of life" when groans and pain accompany loved ones who die in this life. If only we could hear the joy and laughter of Heaven, our pondering and sadness would be transformed into proclaiming and celebrating!

Questions

1. Reminisce about the birth of a child in your life. What were your thoughts? Do you remember the labor pain? Did you notice an arrival of more love as well as the arrival of a baby? Did your life and lifestyle change?

2. What do you imagine it is like in Heaven when a "saint" arrives?

3. Why do you think God came to earth as an infant rather than just "beam" down as a full-grown Savior, ready to preach, teach, heal, and then die on the Cross?

Prayer

Dear Lord, whenever we are tempted to think that miracles do not occur as frequently anymore, please interrupt us with the news of a birth. Then, Lord, let us ponder the miracle, the Holy Moment, and the bridging of the infinite and finite, as You once again grace our world with one of Your handiworks, which we receive and cuddle, and ponder, all in Your most Holy Name. Amen.

Chapter 21
Baptisms

*Do you not know that all of us who have been bap-
tized into Christ Jesus were baptized into his
death? Therefore we have been buried with him
by baptism into death, so that, just as Christ was
raised from the dead by the glory of the Father, so
we too might walk in newness of life. For if we
have been united with him in a death like his, we
will certainly be united with him in a resurrection
like his. We know that our old self was crucified
with him so that the body of sin might be destroyed,
and we might no longer be enslaved to sin ... So
you also must consider yourselves dead to sin and
alive to God in Christ Jesus.*

— Romans 6:3-6, 11

Baptisms are among those Holy Moments in this life that are
effectual but often overlooked in terms of significance. That's why
I see baptisms as Holy Moments. Jesus commands us to baptize.
He sacramentally links his death and resurrection to our baptism in
a way that carries us through his grace into the blessings of forgiveness, life, and eternal salvation. Yet as such miracles occur through
the promise of Jesus, human recipients of baptism often receive the
benefits of baptism unaware — oblivious to the miracle that is occurring, preoccupied with heirloom baptismal gowns, candles, cer-
tificates, and "after church" gatherings. Yet the miracle occurs —
not because we are doing anything ourselves in the baptism, but
simply because Jesus has done it all! We are heirs of his grace,
recipients of his earnings, and benefactors of his benevolence!

Often at baptisms, I marvel at the contrast between the holiness that baptism carries, on the one hand, and the naivete of those
either being baptized or those present at the baptism, on the other

hand. This naivete is not malicious; it is just because of our nature. Yet, our Lord is so good that his promises are just as good as he is even if we do not comprehend the mystery that is occurring in this act that ties us to Christ.

Even if we do not often fully comprehend the holiness of baptism at the time of baptism, the significance of baptism unfolds throughout our lives as we see and experience again and again God's faithfulness, God's grace, and God's promise to rescue, redeem, and redirect us in ways that we can only attribute to our Lord's miraculous presence and activity. The actual event of baptism is a Holy Moment that promises a lifetime of other Holy Moments, followed by an eternity of holiness in the presence Jesus Christ and all the saints.

Questions

1. Reflect upon and discuss the last baptism you attended. Was the holiness of the moment fully appreciated and grasped — or was it "holiness unawares"?

2. What are the advantages — even the possibilities — of grasping the fullness and significance of Holy Moments in contrast to receiving them but not being fully aware of their blessings until later?

3. Discuss Paul's identification of our baptism with the death and resurrection of Jesus Christ.

Prayer

Almighty God, Gracious Father of our Lord Jesus Christ and Author of all Holy Moments in this life and in Heaven forever: We praise and thank You for the precious gift of Holy Baptism and for the miracle that unfolds through this precious gift. Our prayer is that we might more fully grasp the gift so that we can face our futures in the full confidence that we are Your baptized children, and that You will guide, forgive, and keep us, through the promises You offer us, until we see You face to face, in the fulfillment of our baptisms in the final resurrection through Jesus Christ, Your Son, our Lord. Amen.

Chapter 22
My First Experience
With Death

Jesus wept. — John 11:35

My mother died. I was 25 years old. This was my first experience with death — real death. Yes, I knew *of* people who had died before — relatives, people whose deaths were reported on the news, and even a classmate of mine in high school (though there were 900 in our class and I didn't know the person well). My mother's death was my first real experience with death.

Our family had gathered together for her final days as she struggled with cancer. She vacillated between moments of consciousness and drowsiness. We enjoyed and cherished those last several moments of serious communication with her. She knew we loved her. We knew she loved us. We prayed. We laughed. We cried. We waited. Time stopped as we waited. Nothing else in life seemed to matter during those days.

Then she died. We entrusted her to her Savior's care. The funeral came and went; the hurt remained. The void in our lives helped us realize that only the Lord's Spirit and promises can fill the emptiness in our hearts that life reveals. It has been over twenty years since I first came face to face with death. Three passages that were spoken to me during the days immediately following my mother's passing still speak to me:

- "Weeping may linger for the night, but joy comes with the morning" (Psalm 30:5b).
- "Do you not know that all of us who have been baptized into Christ Jesus were baptized into his death? Therefore we have been buried with him by baptism into death, so that, just as Christ was raised from the dead by the glory of the Father, so we too might walk in newness of life. For if

we have been united with him in a death like his, we will certainly be united with him in a resurrection like his" (Romans 6:3-5).

* "If for this life only we have hoped in Christ, we are of all people most to be pitied" (1 Corinthians 15:19).

The reality of my mother's passing to eternal life is just as real today as it was over twenty years ago, but the joy of the Lord has come back into my life! My mother is with the Lord and some day I, too, will rise!

The reality of earthly death has opened my eyes to the even greater reality of eternal life with Jesus Christ. Christ is risen! He is risen indeed!

Questions

1. Share your first real experience with death.

2. Share a promise from God's Word that gives you peace as you think about earthly death.

3. What do you think people will talk about at your memorial service? What would you like them to say at your memorial service? Do you need to make any changes in your life for this to occur?

Prayer

Gracious Heavenly Father, how wonderful it is to know that nothing in all creation can separate us from Your great love given to us through Jesus Christ, Your Son, our Lord — not even death! How wonderful it is that Your Holy Spirit comforts us in our times of bereavement. How wonderful it is that You place people around us, often people from Your Church, who comfort us with the same comfort You have given them in their sorrows. For the Christian, death is but a birth — a birth into eternal life, a birth that is "gain" (Philippians 1:21) because we will be with Christ.

Chapter 23
Walking Away From A Grave

I have fought the good fight, I have finished the race, I have kept the faith. From now on there is reserved for me the crown of righteousness, which the Lord, the righteous judge, will give me on that day, and not only to me but also to all who have longed for his appearing. — 2 Timothy 4:7-8

Over my twenty years of parish ministry, I have compiled a list of the "Top Ten Greatest Joys and the Top Ten Greatest Frustrations in Parish Ministry." The very top joy — almost like an endorphin high — is the feeling I get while walking away from the graveside committal service of a faithful Christian believer. The thought running through my mind at such a time is always the same, "Another one safely home."

The reason this moment is such a joyous and Holy Moment is that the drama is over and the victory is won! Oh, there certainly are many other joys in parish ministry, but most of those other joys are while the drama is still unfolding. Weddings are also joy-filled times, but the drama is far from over for a newlywed couple! Similarly, baptisms are also happy and holy occasions, but, again, what drama lies ahead for both parents and child! The funeral, on the other hand, is holy and complete. The transfer is made. The believer is now "with Christ." Our stewardship of that life is over. At the moment that we give the benediction at a graveside service, we have completed our labors for that person. If that person confessed with his/her lips that Jesus is Lord and believed in his/her heart that God raised Jesus from the dead for our justification, that person is saved! No doubt about it! We have God's Word on it. We can take this promise to the grave — joyously!

As I am walking between the grave site and my car, in addition to thinking, "Another one safely home," I also say a prayer, "Lord, please help me finish well!" So many Christians, like flowers of a field, flourish for a while, but then wither and fade. "Lord, let me please finish like the Apostle Paul, who wrote in 2 Timothy 4:7,' I have fought the good fight, I have finished the race, I have kept the faith. Henceforth, there is laid up for me the crown of righteousness which will be given to me on that Day, and not only to me, but also to all who have longed for his appearing!' " What a joyous and Holy Moment that will be!

Questions

1. Share the thoughts you had between the grave site and your car at the last funeral you attended.

2. Of all the people you know who have died, who among them all are you most certain had a living, saving relationship with Jesus Christ? Does it give you a deep peace knowing that they are *safely home*?

3. What will people be talking about between the grave site and their cars at your graveside service, or between your resurrection celebration (memorial service) and their cars?

Prayer

Almighty God, Gracious Lord and Savior, Thine is the glory, Thine is the victory! Even death loses its sting when You are in our hearts and in our lives! We praise and thank You for all the saints among us who are at this moment safely home. Lord, keep us close to You; keep us hungering and feeding on Your Living Word, until we all safely and peacefully arrive home with You in Heaven through the merit, grace, and mercy of Your Son, Jesus Christ, our Lord. Amen.

Chapter 24
Home Communion

... I was sick and you took care of me ...
— Matthew 25:36

Jesus said, "Where two or three are gathered in my name, there am I in the midst of them" (Matthew 18:20). Most of the times that I bring home communion to homebound members of our church, it is just two, not even three. But there is Jesus in the midst of even just the two of us. With Jesus, we've got three!

What a quiet and Holy Moment home communion is. The Christian being visited is often in a bed or in a recliner. There are signs of the outside world peeking in all around. Some flowers from a neighbor are often on a table. A couple of letters are often out of envelopes and within arm's reach. A telephone is also frequently near. And, even if the pastor were not coming over, a well-worn Bible is near the believer.

Pleasantries are exchanged. Pictures of family in distant cities are often shared. But then, the real reason for the visit becomes obvious to both of us.

I open my communion kit. From a small vial, I pour a little wine into a glass. I take out a wafer and place it on a little plate. It almost looks like play dishes, and play food. But these elements are far from toys! They are *means of grace*. They are, as saints have called them, *food of immortality*. The bread and the wine feed more than the physical body; they also feed and nourish the soul, bring peace to a troubled heart, convey forgiveness to a troubled and penitent heart, and unite the two of us not only with the congregation back at church, but also with the Host of Heaven and the cloud of witnesses! For a moment, Heaven and the promises of Heaven, given to us through Jesus, are present with us! It's a crowd — a joyous crowd — a holy crowd that fills the room!

The benediction is given, a hug and kiss are exchanged. I proceed to my next visit. The homebound believer basks in the holy promises once again spoken and once again believed. And the peace of God rests on that homebound member as the Holy Spirit lingers and ministers.

Questions

1. Share experiences of visiting homebound members of your church.

2. What homebound member of your church will you promise to visit, call, or write this week?

3. What do you think really happens in the Lord's Supper when believers receive it with believing hearts?

Prayer

Almighty and Everlasting Lord, You know the need we humans have for some physical presence and assurance in the midst of our earthly lives. You know this so well that You sent Your one and only Son, Jesus Christ, to visit us, to live among us, to teach us, to embrace us, to heal us, and then to die on the Cross and to rise from the grave — all for us and our salvation. You have also left for us a memorial of Christ's life, death, and resurrection in the gift of the New Passover, the Lord's Supper. We thank and praise You that You have promised that You will be with us always — even when we are homebound, isolated, or feeling very alone — through Your Son, Jesus Christ, our Lord. Amen.

Chapter 25
6 a.m. Bible Study

All scripture is inspired by God and is useful for
teaching, for reproof, for correction, and for train-
ing in righteousness.　　　　— 2 Timothy 3:16

It's strangely enjoyable. Strange, because it is 6 a.m. and way too early to be at church with a group of Bible-toting disciples. Enjoyable, because this small group has bonded through the adversity of rising early and through the joy of studying God's Word together on a weekly basis.

For the past seven years, this 6 to 7 a.m. Thursday morning Bible study has met weekly from September to June. Of the twenty-some participants, there are a handful of veterans who have been part of this early morning Bible study all seven years. A couple of these veterans enjoy the early hour, getting there early enough to open up, turn on the lights and enjoy a cup or two of coffee before the majority punctually arrive at 6 a.m.

The lights in the social hall serve as a warm welcome to those who enter the parking lot while it is still dark. Once inside, the lights, the smell of coffee, and the warm fellowship of this band of people who strangely enjoy this discipline, that borders on the monastic life, spark a liveliness that betrays the early hour. The camaraderie among the early-risers is obvious and warm.

The source of the camaraderie is soon evident. Bibles are opened, prayer is offered, Christ is welcomed, faith is shared, and encouragement is given. The sixty minutes become a single Holy Moment.

After one hour, we break because many of our band need to move on with the day's busy schedule — indeed, their busy schedule is one of the main reasons why they attend this 6 a.m. Bible study instead of the many other Bible studies offered at more normal times.

As we leave the social hall, we experience a parable. The world that was so dark before Bible study is now light. "Thy Word is a lamp to our feet and a light to our path" (Psalm 119:105).

Questions

1. Have you ever shared some "discipline" of discipleship with a group of fellow Christians? (Early Bible study, fasting, prayer group, or mission trip?) If you have, please share your experiences. If you have not, imagine what such an experience would do for you.

2. How important is weekly Bible study for the Christian's life?

3. Granted! It's difficult to get up early. However, it's been said that the best preparation for anything is prayer and Bible study. Discuss how a day goes better when it's been prepared for through Bible study and prayer.

Prayer

Gracious Lord, Your Son often rose while it was still dark so that he could pray and prepare for the events of the day. Prompt us, Lord, to set aside some early morning Holy Moments in prayer and study of Your Holy Word so that we are prepared for the tasks You daily set before us! Then, Lord, just as Moses' face was radiant because he had been talking with You when he came down from the mountain, our faces will radiate the grace, mercy, and peace of Your Son, Jesus Christ, our Lord, with whom we spent some Holy Moments. Amen.

Chapter 26
Cancer

*Even though I walk through the valley of the
shadow of death, I fear no evil; for you are with
me; your rod and your staff — they comfort me.*
— Psalm 23:4

I was 33 when death came knocking at my door. I had just run
in a 10K race a week earlier. I felt fine. I arose and took my usual
morning shower. Even though I am usually in the process of wak-
ing up during my shower, the lump I discovered sent my mind into
a stage one alert. I knew something was wrong. I went to my doc-
tor. He immediately called a specialist and gave me directions to
the specialist's office. The specialist examined me and within fifteen minutes told me that the tumor I found had a 95 percent chance
of being malignant and that we would schedule surgery for the
following day.

My mind was swimming, my heart was sinking, my steps
seemed to be entering the valley of the shadow of death. I was late
for a meeting at church, but stopped by home to tell Cindy, my
wife, the news in person. After relaying to her the information, she
said, "We may not know that the future holds, but we know who
holds the future." She always says the right things!

The next day, I had what turned out to be the first of three
surgeries. It was malignant. The following three months were like
a ride on a roller coaster. The initial pathology report was that,
while it was malignant, it was of the most treatable form of the
type of cancer that I had. Two days later, after more thorough test-
ing, it was discovered that my cancer was the most aggressive strain
of the type of cancer I had.

Initial radiology reports indicated that there was no spread of
the cancer. However, a later biopsy revealed that the cancer had
spread into the lymph system.

The months that followed were filled with two additional surgeries, three courses of chemotherapy, five weeks of hospitalizations, and lots and lots of time in bed.

What Holy Moments I experienced during those weeks and months! Cindy and I had been married for eight years, but never had we spent so much (both in terms of quantity and quality) time together. We prayed; she read Psalms to me. I imagined what would happen to my wife and two children (ages five and two) if I were to die. We bonded with the oncology medical staff and the families of the other cancer patients at the hospital. We grieved with those families when some of their loved ones died.

Never in my life have I experienced the rush of so many Holy Moments in so short a period of time as I experienced during that summer and fall. Jesus was with me. Our conversations were frequent. I was at peace — if I were to die.

But, I didn't die. It is now fifteen years since that summer. For the first ten years following my cancer, I thought about that illness every day. In a strange way, I didn't mind it — it was a reminder that my life is not my own; I have been bought at a price and I really now belong to Christ. Those daily remembrances were always Holy Moments.

For the past several years, I have been able to go a few days in a row without thinking about that experience. I don't like that. Busyness often crowds out Holy Moments — or at least the recognition of them.

Walking through the Valley of the Shadow isn't all bad — if Jesus is walking with you. Indeed, walking through the Valley of the Shadow of death with Jesus is far better than walking oblivious to Jesus in any other place. In other words, if I were to choose between earthly tragedy and trials with many Holy Moments (encounters with Christ) on the one hand and smooth sailing and no or few Holy Moments on the other hand, I'd always choose the walk with the Lord. Wouldn't you?

Questions

1. Discuss your thought process as you decide which you would choose: earthly tragedy and trials with many Holy Moments (encounters with Christ) *or* smooth sailing and no or few Holy Moments.

2. If you were to die today, would your legacy be what you want it to be?

3. Share times in your life when trials or sufferings in your life led to a blessing in your life (James 1:2).

Prayer

Almighty God, Gracious Lord, Great Physician, and Good Shepherd, we praise and thank You for Your goodness, mercy, and compassion. We praise and thank You for Your steadfastness during trials and suffering in this life. You promised that "in this world we will have troubles"; but You also promised that You have "overcome the world." Lord, we trust You above all else. May we dread nothing in life save that of neglecting You and what You have done for us and our salvation. Heighten our sensitivities to Your presence and mercy among us; for it is in those Holy Moments that we are most alive, in Jesus Christ, our Lord. Amen.

Chapter 27
Wednesday Bible Study
Small Group Time

For as the rain and the snow come down from heaven, and do not return there until they have watered the earth, making it bring forth and sprout, giving seed to the sower and bread to the eater, so shall my Word be that goes out from my mouth; it shall not return to me empty, but it shall accomplish that which I purpose, and succeed in the thing for which I sent it. — Isaiah 55:10-11

I know what it's like to be wandering and to have no place to sit or call home. No, I'm not referring to the tragic circumstance of many people in our world who have no home 24 hours a day, seven days a week. I'm referring to the holy hour every Wednesday night when every room in the church, including my office, is full of adult small group Bible studies and youth programs! Not even Sunday morning causes as much of a facilities crush as Wednesday evening Bible study and Kids' Night. (This is partly due to the fact that on Wednesday evening, we have only one time offering Bible study and on Sundays we have multiple services; but a church facility taxed to its limits any time for Christ's purposes always brings goose bumps and a Holy Moment to my soul.)

During this Wednesday evening hour, after the lecture on the Bible lesson for that night and during the time that the adults scatter around our church to meet in their small groups and discuss God's Word in intimate settings, I often walk around the church property basking in the Holy Moment of knowing that God's Word is being planted in the hearts and lives of hundreds of people, young and old. I rejoice in the knowledge that God's Word never returns empty (Isaiah 55:10-11) and that miracles are occurring and will occur in the lives, homes, work places, and neighborhoods of people who are at that moment studying God's Word.

Questions

1. Read Isaiah 55:10-11: "For as the rain and the snow come down from heaven, and do not return there until they have watered the earth, making it bring forth and sprout, giving seed to the sower and bread to the eater, [11] so shall my Word be that goes out from my mouth; it shall not return to me empty, but it shall accomplish that which I purpose, and succeed in the thing for which I sent it."

   Discuss the power of God's Word and the study of God's Word.

2. Share your involvement in and experience with small group Bible study. If you are not presently in a small group Bible study, share with someone else why you are too busy to study God's Word on a weekly basis *or* share with someone else your new commitment to get involved in a weekly Bible study.

3. List the Top Ten Excuses people give for not being in a weekly Bible study. After making the list, consider how Jesus would respond to each excuse.

Prayer

Your Word, O Lord, is a lamp to my feet and a light to my path. Lord, keep me from ever trying to navigate life without the benefit and guidance given by Your Holy Word, the Bible. Please create such an insatiable hunger in my soul for Your Word that I see Bible study as a joy and delight rather than a drudgery or obligation. May Your Word be sweeter to my soul than honey is to my taste! I ask this in the Name of Jesus Christ, the Living Word. Amen.

Chapter 28
Confirmation

"Now therefore revere the Lord, and serve him in sincerity and in faithfulness; put away the gods that your ancestors served beyond the River and in Egypt, and serve the Lord. Now if you are unwilling to serve the Lord, choose this day whom you will serve, whether the gods your ancestors served in the region beyond the River or the gods of the Amorites in whose land you are living; but as for me and my household, we will serve the Lord." Then the people answered, "Far be it from us that we should forsake the Lord to serve other gods; for it is the Lord our God who brought us and our ancestors up from the land of Egypt, out of the house of slavery, and who did those great signs in our sight. He protected us along all the way that we went, and among all the peoples through whom we passed; and the Lord drove out before us all the peoples, the Amorites who lived in the land. Therefore we also will serve the Lord, for he is our God." — Joshua 24:14-18

What makes the Lord the happiest He can be? I think it is when His children (you and I) get a glimpse of Who the Lord really is and somehow express it!

Remember when Jesus questioned the disciples about who people were saying he was? The disciples answered that some thought he was John the Baptist come back to life, others thought he was Elijah, Jeremiah, or one of the other great prophets. (These answers were not bad; they were very complimentary! Jeremiah and Elijah were great prophets!) Then, Jesus directly asked Peter, "What about you; who do you say that I am?"

Peter answered, "You are the Christ, the Son of the Living God!"

You might have thought that Jesus just heard the best news in his entire life! Jesus' response sounded something like, "You're right! You got the question right! Blessed are you, Simon Peter! You listened as my Father in Heaven has taught you!"

Or take another example — my favorite verse from 3 John. "I have no greater joy than to hear that my children are walking in the truth" (3 John 4). While it was the aged John (brother of James and one of the three closest disciples of Jesus) who exclaimed these words, this joy reflects the Lord's elation at when you and I finally "get it" — when finally, with eyes of faith, we see Jesus Christ as God's Son and our Savior!

I think I understand this joy. I have been in confirmation classes with seventh and eighth graders who, in my humble opinion, have not absorbed a single word that I have attempted to teach over the past several months. Then, suddenly, one of them says something, does something, turns in an assignment that evidences that they understand who Jesus Christ is and that they have accepted him as their Lord and Savior. That is a Holy Moment! That Holy Moment makes up for a lot of "other moments" during the confirmation years!

Questions

1. Share a time when you think a confession or expression of faith on your part may have brought joy to Jesus Christ in Heaven.

2. Do you ever feel that some people in church "just don't get it" in terms of who Jesus Christ is and what the Christian life is all about? What keeps us from always behaving and living in ways that evidence that we "get it" all the time?

3. Who can you approach, as Joshua approached the Hebrew people in Joshua 24, and invite to choose the Lord in an intentional way that evidences that they know who Jesus Christ is

and what it means when they say, "As for me, I will serve the Lord!"

Prayer
Almighty God, Savior and Lord, we praise, honor, and glorify You for Your love for, and patience with, us Your children. How often we "just don't get it"! Worse, how often do we have a glimpse of Who You are and we still won't confess or live it! Forgive us, Father. Have patience with us, Lord. Continue to teach us, love us, feed us, and keep asking us who we say You are. Ask us at work, at school, in church, at home, and in our quiet moments. Please be persistent with us. Only through Your persistence are we able finally to make that good confession of faith when we behold You in all Your glory and say, "My Lord and my God!" Then, even You, who are Holy all the time, experience a Holy Moment with us as our faith in You is confirmed and shared, in Jesus' Name. Amen.

Chapter 29
Preschool Chapel

At that time the disciples came to Jesus and asked,
"Who is the greatest in the kingdom of heaven?"
He called a child, whom he put among them, and
said, "Truly I tell you, unless you change and be-
come like children, you will never enter the king-
dom of heaven." — Matthew 18:1-3

Then little children were being brought to him in
order that he might lay his hands on them and pray.
The disciples spoke sternly to those who brought
them; but Jesus said, "Let the little children come
to me, and do not stop them; for it is to such as
these that the kingdom of heaven belongs."
— Matthew 19:13-14

There is a profound difference between being childish and child-like. Children have permission to be both. In children, the first is tolerable but understood, the second is wonderful and too often just envied! Adults, sadly, often do not have permission to be either. In adults, the first (being childish) is neither understood nor tolerated. Lamentingly, the second (being child-like) is also too often neither understood nor tolerated.

Let me share with you a couple of my experiences with doing chapel lessons for preschoolers (three- to five-year-olds); this will teach us what it means to be child-like.

The first example comes from a chapel time that dealt with the Apostle Paul. The students were told that Paul did not always love and serve Jesus. Before Paul met Jesus, he went by the name Saul. Then, after accepting Jesus Christ as his Lord and Savior, this once-mean man became known by another name, Paul, throughout the rest of the Bible. The children were told that often in the Bible, people's names were changed after meeting Jesus because their lives changed so drastically. At this point in the chapel service, little Cliffie raised his hand and said, "Well, then, you can just call me Mike!" What a Holy Moment! That's child-like faith! Cliffie had come to love Jesus and he wanted even his name to reflect this new love!

The second example of child-like faith actually occurred outside of chapel, even outside of the church; but the groundwork for it was laid during preschool chapel. At the end of chapel, we pray for sick and absent students and we sing "Happy Birthday" to students who are celebrating birthdays that week. The preschool version of "Happy Birthday" goes like this (traditional tune):

> *Happy birthday to you! Happy birthday to you!*
> *May Jesus walk with you, this whole year through!*

Just last week, I heard about two of our preschool graduates who had started kindergarten. Someone celebrated a birthday in their class at a local public school. The class sang "Happy Birthday" to the one-year-older child. After the class sang, our two "graduates" looked at each other with puzzled faces and asked the teacher if they could sing their version of happy birthday that they always sang at preschool. The teacher unwittingly agreed. The two children sang their song and blessed not just the birthday-child, but also the whole class! Another Holy Moment! Another example of child-like faith.

Questions

1. How freely do you share your faith in Jesus Christ in public arenas such as at work or in your social circles?

2. Why are children so much more likely to be child-like in their love for and trust in Jesus than adults?

3. What can you do to become more child-like in your relationship to Jesus Christ as your Lord and Savior?

Prayer

Almighty God, Father of our Lord Jesus Christ, and Father of us all, why do we so rebel at seeing ourselves as Your children no matter what age we may be? Why do we so quickly lose that child-like capacity to love freely, witness boldly, and trust completely in You, Lord? We understand that we may lose that capacity toward other humans because they often disappoint us or hurt us, but, Father, You always love us freely and rejoice to see us return love to You in the simplest and purest of ways. Create in us, Father, child-like natures that simply love You, trust You, and rejoice in You every day — to the joy and surprise of everyone around us, in Jesus' Name. Amen!

Chapter 30
Kari's College Letters

I have no greater joy than this, to hear that my
children are walking in the truth. — 3 John 1:4

It was a difficult day — one of the toughest days of our married life. Cindy and I were having difficulty — not with each other, but with the fact that we had just dropped off our daughter, Kari, at college and had just arrived home without her. Sure, I knew that this day was coming. Never, however, had I expected the emotional freight train that hit us that evening. We had her home with us for eighteen years; her bedroom had always been full of light and familiar sounds. Now, it was empty, dark, and quiet.

On the positive side, we were very proud of her. She had graduated as the salutatorian of her class; she was attending a wonderful Christian college; she had a wonderful Christian roommate; she was only forty miles away, for Heaven's sake! Yet her room was dark and we missed her.

Cindy and I did the necessary chores for the evening and prepared for bed. As we turned back the comforter on our bed, there were two envelopes — one on each pillow. They were from Kari. Each note thanked us for preparing her for this special day. Each note contained the holy words, "I love you." Each note comforted us in our tears and loneliness. It was a Holy Moment!

I am writing this chapter two years and two months after that day we first dropped off Kari at college. She is now a junior at that same Christian university. Today, we received a note from Kari. Let me share it with you.

> *Mom and Dad,*
> *I just picked these up for you at Sonshine (a Chris-*
> *tian bookstore) because I want you to know that I re-*
> *ally appreciate your selflessness, encouragement, love,*

and understanding that you've demonstrated to me over the years. I love you! Kari P.S. Have a great week.

Holy Moment! Yes, I will have a great week!

Questions

1. Share the last letter or note you received from someone expressing love, appreciation, or thanks to you. Also share how it made you feel.

2. When was the last time you wrote an appreciative and affection-filled letter to someone in your family?

3. "Therefore encourage one another and build each other up, just as in fact you are doing" (1 Thessalonians 5:11). Discuss the truth of this Bible passage.

Prayer

Gracious Lord, how powerful words are! And why should this surprise us? You spoke the world into existence. Your Son, Jesus Christ, is the Logos, the Word, who became flesh among us to encourage us, to teach us, to die for our sins, to be raised for our justification, and to redeem us. You have sanctified words — both spoken and written by the life of Your Son. Help us, O Lord, to use this gift of words to bless others, to encourage others, to speak to others about You and Your saving activity through Jesus Christ, Your Son, our Lord. Amen.

Chapter 31
In The Shadow

*He (Jesus) must become greater; I must become
less.*   — John 3:30

Three years and four months after the last chapter (in which I
shared the Holy Moments of discovering our daughter's notes under our pillows), my wife and I visited our freshman son on Parents' Weekend at Stanford University. Derek had been there just
four months. Our house was now an "empty nest."

Cindy and I cherish contact-moments with our children, yet
we recognize the necessity of the wing-spreading independence
that must occur as children become adults. Because of this, we
had, all fall, resisted the great temptation to drive up (six and a half
hours) and "pop-in" on Derek and say, "We were in the neighbor-
hood and so we thought we'd just stop by and say hello!" But with
Parents' Weekend, we had a great excuse and opportunity to visit
Derek — on his "home turf."

We arrived late Friday night and enjoyed the couple of hours
we were able to spend with Derek then. Saturday was filled with
typical Parents' Weekend activities: tours of the campus, lunch with
the provost, a couple of athletic events, and assurances from the
administration that our children were safe!

The Holy Moment occurred Sunday morning. Derek wanted
us to pick him up at his dorm at 8:30 a.m. Why? *He was taking us
to his church!* Thus began the Holy Moment. It lasted all morning!

After eighteen years of being brought to Mom and Dad's church
(several times a week as a pastor's kid), he was now bringing us to
his church. We would have been satisfied (ecstatic!) just to go to
worship with him at the church he regularly attended. But, this
wasn't just a church *he regularly attended* — this was *his church*.
Derek took us to his church and to his Sunday school class. We
even had to get there early, so he could show us around *his church*.

We lingered afterward, talking to *his church friends*, both from the church and from his campus. Afterward, he spoke affectionately about his church family. The Holy Moment ended, but the afterglow remained.

The moment reminded me of the time when John the Baptist spoke about Jesus: "He must become greater, I must become less." John was retreating into the shadow as Jesus was becoming the Light! Jesus was replacing Mom and Dad as the reason and motivation for attending church. We were in the shadow. Jesus' influence was becoming greater and Mom and Dad's influence was becoming less. In a way, this was one more bit of evidence that our son was growing up, but to see him growing up into Christ was a fulfilling holy moment!

Questions

1. When you attend church, does it feel like *my church* or just church? Explain.

2. What makes a church *my church*?

3. Share when your faith, along with attending worship, became *your own* and not just a partentally-imposed chore. Or, if attending worship is a chore, what would it take to make church *my church* and to make attending church a joy?

Prayer

Almighty God, Father of our Lord and Savior Jesus Christ, Creator Who blessed the seventh day and made it holy, and Author of the command to remember the Sabbath Day to keep it holy, You are holy! Help us, Lord, to worship You out of a heart's desire rather than just out of an inherited or cultural habit. Let our church family embrace us as we embrace our brothers and sisters in this forever-family of sinners-made-saints, known as the Church, and made holy by the blood of Christ, our Lord. Amen.

Chapter 32
Inadequate Yet Used

*Yet, O Lord, You are our Father; we are the clay,
and You are our potter; we are all the work of your
hand.*   — Isaiah 64:8

*"Can I not do with you, O house of Israel, just as
this potter has done?" says the Lord. "Just like
the clay in the potter's hand, so are you in my hand,
O house of Israel."*   — Jeremiah 18:6

In my more honest moments, I sometimes feel like a specta-
tor! In my more humble moments, I sometimes feel very inadequate and very undeserving of what the Lord does for me, around
me, and, surprisingly, through me.

After I preach a sermon, it amazes me when people say that
something I said deepened their relationship with Jesus Christ. After
a counseling session, it shocks me to hear someone say that I offered the exact advice that was needed to reconcile their marriage.
Weeks after something I don't even remember, it humbles me to
hear people say that some kind deed or word offered by me brought
them out of a downward and dangerous depression and pointed
them to Jesus Christ.

If a piece of common bread used during Holy Communion
could talk, or if water used in a service of Holy Baptism could
speak, or if the donkey that carried Jesus into Jerusalem on Palm
Sunday could converse as did Balaam's donkey (Numbers 22), I
think they might utter the same truth that I am attempting to express in this final chapter. God speaks through imperfect, common, and ordinary means which, in their own right, have no pre-
rogative to be a vehicle of the holy and saving gospel of Jesus
Christ.

95

[Peter said,] *"This Jesus is 'the stone that was rejected by you, the builders; it has become the cornerstone.' There is salvation in no one else, for there is no other name under heaven given among mortals by which we must be saved."*

Now when they saw the boldness of Peter and John and realized that they were uneducated and ordinary men, they were amazed and recognized them as companions of Jesus. — Acts 4:11-13

Why does such a great and perfect God use common, unworthy vessels to bear His message and saving grace to the world? Two reasons. One, because He loves us and He cannot help but meddle in the midst of those whom He loves. Second, because He wants us to make no mistake about Who the real power and agent is behind our all-too-human and imperfect strivings. Hence, our Lord takes vessels inadequate by themselves and then pours His grace, mercy, peace, and salvation into these faith-frigates which carry the gospel into the world. When this happens, nothing less than a Holy Moment occurs — something as common as a bush burns for the Lord and speaks a message that can, by God's power and grace, change the world.

Questions
1. Share an experience when some "ordinary person" spoke a word, did a deed, or came to your rescue in a way that, in some way, "saved" you.

2. Share a time when someone told you that something you did or said dramatically impacted their lives with God's grace.

3. How would you differentiate "coincidence" from "Holy Moments"? Will you express this differentiation the next time you hear the word "coincidence"?

Prayer

Almighty God, Divine Intervener, thank You for never giving up on us. Thank You for pouring Your grace and mercy into the inadequate vessels of our lives and experiences. This flow of Your saving grace and mercy not only redeems lives that are worthless, but also overflows from our redeemed lives in ways that give our lives the awesome privilege of being used in the proclamation and appearing of Your Holy Kingdom. Lord, please give us the honor and privilege of being part of the Holy Moments in which You break into our lost world with the saving Gospel and mercy of Your Son, Jesus Christ, our Lord. Amen!

Holy
Moment
Menagerie

Chapter 33
The Ten Greatest
Frustrations In Ministry

1. Interruptions. How difficult it is to discern which "little foxes" need attention, which should be ignored, and which can ruin the vineyard (Solomon 2:15) if not addressed. It has been said that ministry would be a lot easier if it were not for people and their interruptions. But we always need to remember that *real* ministry often occurs in those interruptions!

2. Administration. Seminary never told us about budgets, bills, and business! Such "structure" to the Church is like a skeleton to a body. Furthermore, following the imagery of 1 Corinthians 12, this part of the body is just as holy and deserves just as worthy-of-Christ-attention as any other part of the one, whole and holy Body of Christ.

3. Too much to do! It isn't so much a case of pursuing planned priorities in parish ministry, but often it becomes "planned neglect." Of what do we need to let go? Sometimes, we need to let go of things that are "good" but not essential if keeping the "good" means that the essential (Christ and the Word) will be neglected.

4. Cattiness. How mean church members can be to one another! Does anything grieve our Lord's heart more than this?

5. The penultimate. The penultimate is something that is just less than the ultimate. It constantly vies to usurp the ultimate. In many of C. S. Lewis' writings, the danger of the penultimate usurping the ultimate is warned against more than the danger of overt evil overtaking us. Overt evil is easy to spot and it is easy to know what our response to it should be. The penultimate, however, is always good, noble, nice, attractive, and very easy to mistake as the ultimate. The penultimate, however, is never the ultimate; only Jesus Christ is the ultimate.

6. Confirmation. Just like a future disciple once asked, "Can anything good come out of Nazareth?" many ask, "Can anything good come out of confirmation classes?" The answer, of course, is come and see. Confirmation is one of the most frustrating and difficult teaching times in the church, yet it is also one of the most fulfilling and miracle-witnessing events in a pastor's life.

7. Divisions and factions. The Apostle Paul identified this frustration in 1 Corinthians 1 when he wrote, "Is Christ divided?" How sad it is when we major in minors, dividing the Church and wasting the Church's energies on divisions based on personalities, styles of worship, aesthetics, self-justifying interpretations of the Bible, and so on.

8. After school sports and activities. Why do families commit to never missing a practice or a game and yet have what appears to be a cavalier attitude toward worship or Bible class attendance even when they know in their heart of hearts that, as the Bible says, "Physical training has some value, but Godliness is of greatest value" (1 Timothy 4:8)?

9. Falls from grace. How it hurts the credibility and witness of Christ's Church when Christians, especially leaders and pastors, fall from grace. Second Timothy 4:7 calls us to finish well!

10. Myself. My human sinfulness, for which I daily repent and against which my new life in Christ struggles, stains the purity of Christ's gospel as I try to deliver it daily. My inept and flat-out inability to do well that which the Lord calls me to do frustrates me. My reluctance to die to self and find new birth in Christ daily and joyfully in the way that Galatians 2:20 invites me does nothing but limit my ministry.

Chapter 34
The Ten Greatest Joys In Ministry

1. Walking from the grave side of a believer's funeral ... thinking, "Another one safely home."

2. Small group time during midweek Bible study ... when every room of the church is full of people (children and adults) in small groups studying God's Word. What a joyous wonder that people will come to study God's Word!

3. Walking person to person, at the altar rail, during Holy Communion distribution ... serving the Living Bread from Heaven to people I know intimately well — from a widow still grieving the loss of her husband, to a young couple celebrating the birth of a new baby.

4. Baptisms, home communions, and weddings. What a joy and privilege it is to be part of these Holy Moments in so many people's lives!

5. Hearing one's own child (in our case, two PKs — pastor's kids) express his/her *own* faith. Third John 4 says, "I have no greater joy than to hear that my children are walking in the Truth."

6. The closing hymn of the last Easter or Christmas service and the first two hours afterward ... basking in the holy afterglow of God's people at worship. Similar to the hormone-induced high a runner feels at the end of a race, there is a spiritual high that accompanies the end of an exhausting effort fully given to the Lord.

7. Preschool chapel. How receptive and open preschoolers' hearts are to the gospel! Jesus said, "Unless you change and become like children, you will never enter the kingdom of heaven" (Matthew 18:3).

8. When a confirmation student "lights" up with Christ — or is even curious about Christ ... I rejoice, I celebrate, I praise the Lord. Yes, good does come out of confirmation classes — and out of every sowing of the Word! "God's Word does not return empty" (Isaiah 55:10-11).

9. Hospital calls ... to people who, in their hospital gowns, are stripped of pretense and all earthy security, who know their absolute dependence upon God's grace offered through Jesus Christ, and who receive God's Word as the medicine of immortality in their hour of need.

10. Any time I feel inadequate but used by Christ, such as when a sermon I pored over (and it remained poor) is used by our Lord anyhow; or when a counseling session occurs wherein God's grace is more active than my words; or when a miracle occurs in spite of me and my faith.

Chapter 35
My 66 Favorite Bible Verses

Old Testament

Genesis 50:20 "Even though you intended to do harm to me, God intended it for good, in order to preserve a numerous people, as he is doing today."

Exodus 34:29 "As he came down from the mountain with the two tablets of the covenant in his hand, Moses did not know that his face was radiant because he had been talking with God."

Leviticus 16:22 "The goat will carry on itself all their sins to a solitary place."

Numbers 21:9 "So Moses made a serpent of bronze, and put it upon a pole; and whenever a serpent bit someone, that person would look at the serpent of bronze and live."

Deuteronomy 31:8 "It is the Lord who goes before you. He will be with you; he will not fail you or forsake you. Do not fear or be dismayed."

Joshua 24:15 "Now if you are unwilling to serve the Lord, choose this day whom you will serve, whether the gods your ancestors served in the region beyond the River or the gods of the Amorites in whose land you are living; but as for me and my household, we will serve the Lord."

Judges 6:13 "Gideon answered, 'But sir, if the Lord is with us, why then has all this happened to us?' "

Ruth 1:16 "Do not press me to leave you or to turn back from following you! Where you go, I will go; where you lodge, I will lodge; your people shall be my people, and your God my God."

1 Samuel 16:7 "The Lord does not see as mortals see; they look on the outward appearance, but the Lord looks on the heart."

2 Samuel 24:24 "King David said to Araunah, 'No, I insist on buying them from you for a price; I will not offer burnt offerings to the Lord my God that cost me nothing.' "

1 Kings 19:18 "Yet I will reserve seven thousand in Israel, all the knees that have not bowed to Baal, and every mouth that has not kissed him."

2 Kings 18:4 "Hezekiah broke in pieces the bronze serpent that Moses had made, for until those days the people of Israel had made offerings to it; it was called Nehushtan."

1 Chronicles 29:14 "But who am I, and what is my people, that we should be able to make this freewill offering? For all things come from you, and of your own have we given you."

2 Chronicles 20:12 "We are powerless against this great multitude that is coming against us. We do not know what to do, but our eyes are on you."

Ezra 9:10 "And now, our God, what shall we say after this? For we have forsaken your commandments."

Nehemiah 6:3 "I sent messengers to Sanballat and Geshem with this reply: 'I am carrying on a great project and cannot go down.' "

Esther 4:14 "Who knows? Perhaps you have come to royal dignity for just such a time as this."

Job 1:21 "Naked I came from my mother's womb, and naked shall I return there; the Lord gave, and the Lord has taken away; blessed be the name of the Lord."

Psalm 119:105 "Your word is a lamp to my feet and a light to my path."

Proverbs 3:5-6 "Trust in the Lord with all your heart, and do not rely on your own insight. In all your ways acknowledge him, and he will make straight your paths."

Ecclesiastes 12:13 "The end of the matter; all has been heard. Fear God, and keep his commandments; for that is the whole duty of everyone."

Solomon 2:15 "Let us catch the foxes, the little foxes that ruin the vineyards — for our vineyards are in blossom."

Isaiah 53:6 "All we like sheep have gone astray; we have all turned to our own way; the Lord has laid on him the iniquity of us all."

Jeremiah 29:13 "When you search for me, you will find me; if you seek me with all your heart."

Lamentations 3:23 "Thy mercies are new every morning; great is thy faithfulness."

Ezekiel 22:30 "I looked for a man among them who would build up the wall and stand before me in the gap on behalf of the land so I would not have to destroy it, but I found none."

Daniel 3:18 "But if not, be it known, O king, that we will not serve your gods and we will not worship the golden statue that you have set up."

Hosea 14:4 "I will heal their waywardness and love them freely, for my anger has turned away from them."

Joel 2:13 "Rend your hearts and not your clothing. Return to the Lord, your God, for he is gracious and merciful, slow to anger, and abounding in steadfast love, and relents from punishing."

Amos 7:8 "The Lord said, 'See, I am setting a plumb line in the midst of my people Israel; I will never again pass them by.' "

Obadiah 1:4 "Though you soar aloft like the eagle, though your nest is set among the stars, from there I will bring you down, says the Lord."

Jonah 1:2 "Go at once to Nineveh, that great city, and cry out against it; for their wickedness has come up before me."

Micah 7:7 "But as for me, I will look to the Lord, I will wait for the God of my salvation; my God will hear me."

Nahum 1:7 "The Lord is good, a refuge in times of trouble. He cares for those who trust in him."

Habakkuk 3:18 "Yet I will rejoice in the Lord; I will exult in the God of my salvation."

Zephaniah 3:9 "At that time I will change the speech of the peoples to a pure speech, that all of them may call on the name of the Lord and serve him with one accord."

Haggai 1:7 "Thus says the Lord of hosts: 'Consider how you have fared.' "

Zechariah 14:9 "And the Lord will become king over all the earth; on that day the Lord will be one and his name the only name."

Malachi 3:8 "Will anyone rob God? Yet you are robbing me! But you say, 'How are we robbing you?' In your tithes and offerings!"

New Testament
Matthew 6:33 "Seek first his kingdom and his righteousness, and all these things will be given to you as well."

Mark 14:8 "She has done what she could; she has anointed my body beforehand for its burial."

Luke 11:28 "But Jesus said, 'Blessed rather are those who hear the word of God and obey it!' "

John 16:33 "In this world you will have trouble, but take heart, I have overcome the world."

Acts 17:11 "Now the Bereans were of more noble character than the Thessalonians, for they received the message with great eagerness and examined the scriptures every day to see if what Paul said was true."

Romans 8:28 "We know that all things work together for good for those who love God, who are called according to his purpose."

1 Corinthians 2:2 "For I decided to know nothing among you except Jesus Christ, and him crucified."

2 Corinthians 5:21 "For our sake God made him to be sin who knew no sin, so that in him we might become the righteousness of God."

Galatians 2:20 "I have been crucified with Christ, and it is no longer I who live, but it is Christ who lives in me. The life I now live in the flesh I live by faith in the Son of God, who loved me and gave himself for me."

Ephesians 2:10 "For we are God's handiwork, created in Christ Jesus for good works, which God prepared beforehand to be our way of life."

Philippians 4:4 "Rejoice in the Lord always; again I will say, Rejoice."

Colossians 3:17 "In whatever you do, in word or deed, do everything in the name of the Lord Jesus, giving thanks to God the Father through him."

1 Thessalonians 5:16-18 "Rejoice always, pray without ceasing, give thanks in all circumstances; for this is the will of God in Christ Jesus for you."

2 Thessalonians 3:1 "Brothers and sisters, do not be weary in doing what is right."

1 Timothy 4:1 "Let no one despise your youth, but set the believers an example in speech and conduct, in love, in faith, in purity."

2 Timothy 3:16 "All scripture is inspired by God and is useful for teaching, for reproof, for correction, and for training in righteousness."

Titus 2:1 "But as for you, teach what is consistent with sound doctrine."

Philemon 1:6 "I pray that you may be active in sharing your faith, so that you will have a full understanding of every good thing we have in Christ."

Hebrews 12:1 "Therefore, since we are surrounded by so great a cloud of witnesses, let us also lay aside every weight and the sin that clings so closely, and let us run with perseverance the race that is set before us, keeping our eyes fixed on Jesus."

James 1:19 "Let everyone be quick to listen, slow to speak, slow to anger."

1 Peter 5:7 "Cast all your anxiety on him, because he cares for you."

2 Peter 3:9 "The Lord is not slow about his promise, as some think of slowness, but is patient with you, not wanting any to perish, but all to come to repentance."

1 John 4:7-8 "Beloved, let us love one another, because love is from God; everyone who loves is born of God and knows God. Whoever does not love does not know God, for God is love."

2 John 1:4 "I was overjoyed to find some of your children walking in the truth, just as we have been commanded by the Father."

3 John 1:4 "I have no greater joy than this, to hear that my children are walking in the truth."

Jude 1:22 "Have mercy on those who are wavering."

Revelation 3:20 "Behold! I stand at the door and knock. If anyone hears my voice and opens the door, I will come in and eat with him, and he with me."